The Bible and Gender-based Violence in Botswana

The Bible and Gender-based Violence in Botswana foregrounds the rampancy of gender-based violence against women and girls in biblical texts and how it resonates with gender-based violence (GBV) in the author's contemporary context of Botswana.

The volume reads selected texts from the Bible alongside newspaper reports of GBV against women and girls in Botswana to show that while the Bible is taken as an authoritative text within the Botswana context, it is riddled with GBV against female persons. It asserts that by acknowledging and naming GBV in biblical texts and not concealing, ignoring, or spiritualizing it, contemporary communities of faith will be able to confront the problem in these contexts. By so doing, the book argues, the Bible will become a resource for positive transformation rather than a tool for supporting gender injustice.

The book appeals to everyone willing to see positive change in regard to gender in/equality and is intended for a wide readership including researchers, postgraduates, church and other representatives of religious institutions, and upper-level undergraduates.

Mmapula Diana Kebaneilwe is a Senior Lecturer of the Hebrew Bible at the University of Botswana. She is a Humboldtian Research Fellow in Germany and the author of "Jesus as a Victim of Sexual Abuse" in Reaves, J., Tombs, D. and Figueroa, R. (Eds.), *When Did We See You Naked* (2021).

Rape Culture, Religion and the Bible
Series Editors:
Caroline Blyth, *University of Auckland, New Zealand*
Johanna Stiebert, *University of Leeds, UK*

Rape Culture, Purity Culture, and Coercive Control in Teen Girl Bibles
Caroline Blyth

Trafficking Hadassah
Collective Trauma, Cultural Memory, and Identity in the Book of Esther and in the African Diaspora
Ericka Shawndricka Dunbar

Vocation and Violence
The Church and #MeToo
Miryam Clough

Zeus Syndrome
A Very Short History of Religion-Based Masculine Domination
Joachim Kügler

The Crucifixion of Jesus
Torture, Sexual Abuse, and the Scandal of the Cross
David Tombs

Marriage, Bible, Violence
Intersections and Impacts
Saima Afzal and Johanna Stiebert

The Bible and Gender-based Violence in Botswana
Mmapula Diana Kebaneilwe

For more information about this series, please visit: https://www.routledge.com/Rape-Culture-Religion-and-the-Bible/book-series/RCRB

The Bible and Gender-based Violence in Botswana

Mmapula Diana Kebaneilwe

LONDON AND NEW YORK

First published 2024
by Routledge
4 Park Square, Milton Park, Abingdon, Oxon OX14 4RN

and by Routledge
605 Third Avenue, New York, NY 10158

Routledge is an imprint of the Taylor & Francis Group, an informa business

© 2024 Mmapula Diana Kebaneilwe

The right of Mmapula Diana Kebaneilwe to be identified as author of this work has been asserted in accordance with sections 77 and 78 of the Copyright, Designs and Patents Act 1988.

All rights reserved. No part of this book may be reprinted or reproduced or utilised in any form or by any electronic, mechanical, or other means, now known or hereafter invented, including photocopying and recording, or in any information storage or retrieval system, without permission in writing from the publishers.

Trademark notice: Product or corporate names may be trademarks or registered trademarks, and are used only for identification and explanation without intent to infringe.

British Library Cataloguing-in-Publication Data
A catalogue record for this book is available from the British Library

Library of Congress Cataloging-in-Publication Data
Names: Kebaneilwe, Mmapula Diana, author.
Title: The Bible and gender-based violence in Botswana / Mmapula Diana Kebaneilwe.
Description: New York : Routledge, 2024. | Includes bibliographical references and index. | Identifiers: LCCN 2023054861 | Subjects: LCSH: Bible--Criticism, interpretation, etc. | Bible--Influence. | Gender-based violence--Religious aspects--Christianity. | Gender-based violence--Botswana. | Sex role--Biblical teaching. | Women--Violence against--Botswana. | Women--Botswana--Social conditions.
Classification: LCC HV6626.23.B55 K433 2024 | DDC 362.8292096883--dc23
LC record available at https://lccn.loc.gov/2023054861

ISBN: 978-1-032-10192-7 (hbk)
ISBN: 978-1-032-10194-1 (pbk)
ISBN: 978-1-003-21413-7 (ebk)

DOI: 10.4324/9781003214137

Typeset in Times New Roman
by KnowledgeWorks Global Ltd.

This book is dedicated to the countless women and girls who have lost their lives, suffered injuries, lived, and continue to live difficult lives simply because they are female. May God grant all women and girls a relentless spirit to challenge gender-based violence that comes to them in all forms. May they speak like Esther: "If I perish, I perish" (Esther 4:16).

Contents

Acknowledgments   ix

1   A Contextual Background   1

   Defining Gender-based Violence 3
   What Is Botswana Like? A Brief Background 4
   "A Woman Is [Like] a Baboon" 7
   "Women Are [Like] Cows and Cannot Lead" 9
   The Socio-political and Cultural Landscape of Botswana:
     Past and Present 11
   Protection from Discrimination Based on Gender 13
   Domestic Violence Act (2008) 14
     The Botswana Penal Code Amendment 16
     The Sexual Harassment Act 16
     The Abolition of Marital Power Act (2004) 17
   The Religious Landscape of Botswana:
     Spiritualization of Patriarchy 19
   Conclusion 24
   Notes 25
   Bibliography 26

2   Establishing the Gaps: The Bible and GBV in Context   32

   GBV in the Bible: The Quest for Transformational
     Revelation 32
   The Ujamaa Centre: South Africa and Biblical
     Contextualization for Transformation 33
   What Has Preceded: Efforts to Confront the Patriarchal
     Status Quo in Both the Bible and Setswana Culture 38

No Recycling of Biblical Injustices: Read It,
  Name It, and Fix It 43
Notes 44
Bibliography 46

3 Gender-based Violence: Endemic in Biblical Texts
   and in Botswana Context   49

   Genesis 1–3: The Beginning of Deposition of
     Females—and of GBV 52
   Eve and GBV: The Embodiment of a Fallen
     Model for All Women 54
     An Archetype 54
   Grabbing of Vaginas: 2 Samuel 13 and Rape
     Narratives from Botswana 56
   The Book of Esther and GBV in Botswana: Silencing,
     Barred Choices, and Banishments 61
   Objectification and Sexualization: Female Bodies
     for Male Desire and Gratification 64
   In Dire Situations Women's Bodies Became Spaces
     of Contention: The Many Faces of GBV in Both
     the Bible and Botswana 66
   Conclusions towards Solutions 69
   Notes 71
   Bibliography 73

4 A Way Forward   78

   An Imaginary World with Real People in It: The Bible
     and the Contemporary World 78
   Note 84
   Bibliography 84

Index   *86*

Acknowledgments

I am deeply indebted to a special woman who is my teacher, friend, mentor, and confidante-Professor Johanna Stiebert. This book would probably never have seen the light if it were not for her encouragement, guidance, love, and support. Johanna's meticulous editing with such precision made this book more readable than it would have been. I would also love to thank Dr Katie Edwards, with whom Johanna and I did the initial research on "Resisting Gender-based Violence through the Bible and its Images," funded by the Arts and Humanities Research Council (AHRC), to whom I would also love to extend my gratitude.

I also thank the Alexander von Humboldt Foundation for the Research Fellowship that enabled me to concentrate on the writing of this book. I am especially grateful to Professor Joachim Kügler of the University of Bamberg for hosting me as a Humboldtian during this time. His friendship and hospitality made my stay in Germany worthwhile and fun. Last but not least, I thank the University of Botswana for allowing me a year of sabbatical leave to pursue my research and writing.

Finally, I want to thank my personal person, D.K.W. Reschke, for your companionship; those special moments and the laughter we shared made writing this book more enjoyable. Your love lightens up my life and gives me hope for the future.

1 A Contextual Background

My title, *The Bible and Gender-based Violence in Botswana*, is suggestive of two things: First, that there is a possible relationship, connection, or collusion between the Bible and gender-based violence in Botswana and, second, that the Bible might possibly be used as a tool to address gender-based violence in this context. Indeed, this book aims to explore both the possibility that the Bible is not blameless in some incidences of gender-based violence *and* that the same Bible holds potential to be used to resist, address, and curb gender-based violence (henceforth, GBV).

This book pays special attention to and focuses on Botswana, my own situational context. The Bible, as the sacred text of Christianity, the country's dominant religion, occupies a special place in the lives of many people in Botswana who intimately associate themselves with its faith and teachings. This has been proven by previous research, which shows that more than 70% of Botswana's population subscribe to Christianity (CIA World Fact Book).[1] Nevertheless, it will not surprise that the initial idea I presented here, that the Bible plays some negative influence in issues of gender inequality and GBV, directly or indirectly, intentionally, or otherwise, is seen as problematic by many Christian adherents in Botswana who cherish the Bible. This is in part because it is common practice, as in many communities of faith, to treat sacred texts as authoritative and not to be questioned. Indeed, the authority of the Bible is widely accepted at face value and as setting a blueprint and providing a manual for life. Therefore, suggesting that it is possible for the Bible to contribute to social ills, such as GBV, is problematic and not easily accepted by many communities of faith, including in Botswana.

The second suggestion, that the Bible can set the ethical record straight and prevent or facilitate healing for GBV, is likely to be viewed more favorably. The idea that the Bible can right wrongs and achieve social justice is more conventional and acceptable. In this book, however, I seek to do both: That is, to explore heuristic ways of reading and interpreting the Bible, which expose negative influences of the Bible on gender inequality and, subsequently, GBV, and which address the ongoing GBV pandemic in Botswana.

To be more specific: This is personal to me. As a Motswana[2] woman—a mother, grandmother, divorcee, and scholar of the Bible—the current GBV

DOI: 10.4324/9781003214137-1

crisis in my country is of urgent concern to me for subjective and for professional reasons. In this book, I draw on my research, experiences, and identity to explore how the Bible and the faith communities in Botswana it inspires intersect with traditional and political landscapes to reinforce rape culture and gender inequality, focusing especially on GBV. I identify the religious roots of GBV in present-day Botswana and consider ways in which biblical scholarship can work to resist this scourge. In a country that is so prominently Bible-believing, grisly, heinous, and despicable forms of gender inequality and GBV continue to stifle women and their potential. This cannot be ignored. There is a glaring need to explore the intersections of Setswana traditional and religious culture with Christianity, as the two sit together side by side in the toxic environment characterized by rape culture and its manifestations of GBV.

Violence in Botswana is gendered, disproportionately affecting women and girls. Neither in Botswana can feel safe, not even in their homes, due to the rampant violence targeting them from multiple sides. For instance, rates of GBV are incredibly high; women and girls are raped by their husbands, intimate partners, relatives, strangers, you name it. Men and boys abuse women and girls emotionally and verbally even as they try to go about their regular lives, carrying out their daily activities, at their workplaces or on the street. This is because, as is typical of rape cultures, sexual violence is founded on microaggressions. Hence, women and girls commonly get whistled at, to get their attention, and, when they turn to look, some random man or boy says something sexually loaded, suggesting that in seeing a woman or girl, they see a sexual object.[3] Batswana males (boys and men) freely use derogatory comments towards women, whether they know them or not, often without any instigation. Even boys, young enough to be their female target's son or grandson, will say what they want, showing no regard for her feelings, let alone any sense of respect. As rates of many crimes skyrocket in Botswana, due to a combination of factors, including high unemployment levels, high numbers of economic migrants from troubled neighbor countries of the continent, and the escalating cost of living, women are disproportionately affected by the rise in crime, including GBV.[4]

The idea I want to convey is that Botswana's women are acutely vulnerable. The country may be imagined as irenic and benign, given the internationally known depictions of the popular and acclaimed *The No. 1 Ladies Detective Agency* series of books by Alexander McCall Smith and the charming TV adaptation that followed it. The books put Botswana on the international radar, presenting it as a sleepy, friendly place. Otherwise, Botswana is famous in the Western world above all for its safari tourism and diamonds. It is widely regarded as a stable and successful economy and democracy. While there is some truth in all these assessments, that is also not the whole truth. Hence, the rising statistics of GBV tell a different, much more somber story. In Botswana, women are attacked in their cars and bedrooms; they are prone to harassment even in busy shopping malls. Women get killed by their husbands, ex-husbands, lovers, and ex-lovers in what is notoriously known in the country as "passion killings" (Ellece and Rapoo 2013; Exner and Thurston 2009). Such killings are predominantly of women, while perpetrators are almost exclusively male. Such accounts may be familiar from South Africa where reports show that the country has the highest incidence of rape cases outside of a war zone in the world, with a shocking 10,818 rape cases recorded in the first quarter of 2022.[5] Sadly, Botswana shares high incidence of sexual violence with its neighbor.

This is reality in Botswana, too—even if this is far less widely acknowledged in either Botswana itself or internationally. For instance, even though Botswana lacks official GBV statistics, as these are omitted in the country's demographic surveys, the World Population Review (2023) identifies Botswana as number one in the world in incidences of rape at 92.93% per 100,000 people. Moreover, the likelihood is that actual cases far exceed this, given that GBV is generally underreported for several reasons, including stigmatization of victims and fear of reprisals (see Koss 1993; Mooketsane et al. 2023).

What can we make of such despicable harm inflicted on women and girls? After all, this is happening in a predominantly Christian context, where we might have expected a Christian ethos and Christian values to facilitate peace and compassion. As a starting point, a brief overview of present-day Botswana that aims to orient and acquaint the reader with an understanding of the context of this book will follow. But before that, a definition of GBV is in order, to lay the foundation for how I understand the term and how it relates to the biblical texts to be examined.

Defining Gender-based Violence

GBV refers to violence perpetrated against a person based, to some extent at least, on the person's gender or violence that disproportionately affects persons of a particular gender. Anyone, women, girls, men, and boys, as well as persons of non-binary or trans gender, can become a victim of GBV. Women and girls are the largest group affected by GBV (United Nations Refugee Agency).

GBV against women has been defined as any act that results in or is likely to cause physical, sexual, or psychological harm to them. Threats of violence, coercion, or arbitrary deprivation of liberty and manipulation in public and private life also constitute GBV (United Nations 1995, Platform for Action D. 112). GBV is complex, manifests in different forms, and affects those afflicted differently. The UN General Assembly (1993) indicated some ways in which GBV targeting women and girls manifests itself, and the list includes physical, sexual, and psychological violence within the family, child sexual abuse, dowry-related violence, marital rape female genital mutilation, rape and sexual abuse, sexual harassment in the workplace and educational institutions, trafficking and forced prostitution e.t.c..

In this book, I explore GBV against first, textual-biblical women as inscribed within the Bible and second, Batswana women. As indicated, the aim is not just to expose the abovementioned forms of GBV perpetrated against these women but to seek ways to address them, especially using the same Bible.

Importantly, as we shall see in this book, GBV is rooted and thrives in contexts where women are subordinated to men. Even seemingly progressive laws often do little to mitigate this. For instance, in South Africa, which has an unusually progressive constitution, there is a great deal of sexual violence with reports showing that one in three South African women will be raped in their lifetime (Moffet 2009, 155). Botswana too has laws on sexual violence, and I will later discuss those and their failure to prevent widespread sexual crimes. In such contexts, GBV is often tacitly condoned by institutions and cultural traditions and norms that discriminate against women and girls (Heise, Ellsberg and Gottemoeller 1999 cited by Bott, Morrison and Ellsberg 2005). The same is true for both the world presented by and in the Bible and for Botswana—past and present. These ideas will be explored further as the book unfolds.

What Is Botswana Like? A Brief Background

Botswana is a land-locked country situated along the Tropic of Capricorn in the central part of southern Africa, sharing borders with South Africa to the south and southeast, Namibia to the west, and Zambia and Zimbabwe to the north and northeast. The country is approximately 581,730 square km of land (or 224,607 square miles), which is the size of Texas (USA), and slightly bigger than France (Quansah 2008, 489). The country is ethnically speaking fairly homogenous with the bulk of the population being native Batswana of African descent, mostly of the southern Bantu group related to the people of Lesotho and parts of South Africa (Quansah 2008). There are also the San people, generally "considered the first inhabitants of Southern Africa and their population spreads throughout four countries today. The San people are now found in parts Botswana, South Africa, Namibia, and Angola" (Lebotse 2009, 26). The San are only a small minority of about 3.3% of the population of Botswana (Hitchcock 2002, 798). Aside from this, the population includes small minorities of Europeans (mainly of British and Afrikaans descent), and Asians (mainly of Indian and Chinese descent; Quansah 2008). As further noted by Emmanuel Quansah,

> The social and cultural values of the country are embodied in four principles, namely, (1) democracy (*puso ya batho ka batho*); (2) development (*ditiro tsa ditlhabololo*); (3) self-reliance (*boipelego*); and (4) unity (*popagano ya sechaba*). These principles are derived from traditional culture and are designed to promote social harmony (*kagisano*).
>
> (Quansah 2008, 489)

Two-thirds of the country is covered by the Kalahari Desert, while the Okavango Delta in the north forms a large in-land delta, which is home to a vast variety of wildlife that congregates there (Denbow and Thebe 2006). Wildlife makes the Okavango Delta, like some other parts of the country, a desirable tourist destination, attracting multitudes of visitors from around the world, except during the COVID-19 pandemic, when tourism terminated.

Many of Botswana's 2,675,352 inhabitants[6] live in the eastern part of the country where farming is made possible by fertile soils and seasonal rainfall (Denbow et al. 2006). Although the country has a relatively small population of under 3 million, this is made up of multiple African ethnic sub-groups with diverse languages, traditions, cultures, and religions (Togarasei 2013, 3). There are also, however, similarities and cultural affinities between these groups, permitting some degree of generalization. English and Setswana (Setswana being the dominant indigenous language) are the country's two official languages.

A former British Protectorate, Botswana became independent from Britain on 30 September 1966. At the point of independence, Botswana was among the poorest and least developed countries in the world, inheriting close to nothing in terms of physical and social infrastructure from colonial rule (Owusu and Samatar 1997). Very few Batswana had higher education at this time: There were just 40 university graduates and about 100 high school leavers at independence, a situation again blamed on the colonial government's neglect (Siphambe 2000). After gaining independence, the country embarked on its journey towards self-sufficiency and food security (Magang 2015). Botswana went on to make history by becoming a middle-income country and one of the fastest-growing economies in Africa and beyond—not least, on account of the discovery of diamonds, soon after gaining independence. The country embarked also on ambitious education campaigns. Today Botswana prides herself on free and inclusive education (Lekoko and Maruatona 2006). This has seen many Batswana acquire high levels of education, and I am a beneficiary of such a privilege myself.

To fast-forward, Botswana of the present boasts considerable economic growth, relative peace and stability, parliamentary democracy with regular elections, and comparative security when viewed alongside her neighbors, such as South Africa and Zimbabwe, not to mention other war-torn countries on the continent, such as the Democratic Republic of Congo and North and South Sudan. The country ranks high in sub-Saharan Africa not just in terms of income per capita but also in terms of indicators of human development, including public expenditure on health and education (Good, 1993). Botswana is further lauded for her democratic government, low levels of corruption, and independent judiciary, again comparing favorably with many other African nation states (Cailleba and Kumar 2010, 330). Although from 1966 to this day the Botswana Democratic Party (BDP) has been the only governing party in the country, Botswana holds elections every five years and there exist several opposition parties in the country. However, Botswana is also characterized by inequalities where the pronounced gap between the richest and poorest is concerned as well as by gender inequality. One study shows that women are paid less than men despite being on average more highly educated (Siphambe 2000). These issues and more will be discussed shortly.

It is noteworthy to mention that Botswana's geographical position at the center of southern Africa, coupled with her status as a peaceful, relatively stable economy, brings its own challenges. One of these challenges is that of undocumented economic immigration, particularly from Zimbabwe and Mozambique (Campbell 2006, 2). For instance, due to the economic crisis in Zimbabwe since the 1990s, Botswana has grappled with an influx of economic migrants (Ibid). Moreover, the predicament of undocumented migrants in southern Africa more generally has not only affected Botswana but two other countries with relatively favorable economic environments in the region as well: Namely, South Africa and Namibia (Campbell 2006, 2). Botswana has experienced an increasing rate of crime in recent times, and this has partly been blamed on undocumented migrants. In some cases, such migrants have also been scapegoats for criminal activities, including robberies, house break-ins, rapes, and killings.

With women and girls being frequent targets of rape and frequent victims of killings, we see in newspaper headlines, on national television, and social media platforms how women's and girls' bodies have become spaces of contention, including in blaming violence on perceived outsiders. With economic downturn troubling much of the world, and with Africa the hardest hit, women have borne the brunt of all sorts of violence, much of it at the hands of men. This is true also of Botswana where I live and teach biblical studies. GBV in my country and the complex webs of connection I see, including webs incorporating religion (which is a powerful force in Botswana, as shall be discussed shortly), are what have prompted the writing of this book.

Botswana's successes should not distract attention away from some of the very real and harmful socio-economic, political, and social challenges with which the country is battling. Both international and domestic comparisons show up sharp inequalities of wealth and income, making the disparities between the very rich and the very poor pronounced, systemic, and growing (Good, 1993). Sadly, income inequality in Botswana is also a gendered phenomenon, with women and girls representing a majority in the poorest sectors (Lekobane and Mooketsane 2015).

As noted by Ncube, Lufumpa, and Vencatachellum, in Botswana, as in other parts of the world, women have had dual roles as professionals and mothers/wives and caretakers, and this has not only contributed to gender inequality in the household but also in the labor market as well as in women's lower social positions and in costs to their health and well-being (Ncube et.al. 2011, 3). While in developed countries gender parity in the household has evolved somewhat, gender inequality remains a profound challenge in Botswana, and for sub-Saharan Africa, very little has been achieved (Ncube et.al.

2011, 4). In Botswana, women's potential remains negatively impacted, and they have considerably lower levels of income than men (see Gobagoba and Littrell 2003; Ntseane 2004). That is, gender inequality has afforded men an advantage over women (Owusu and Samatar 1997). Consequently, "Botswana's much talked about 'economic miracle' status has not translated into the reduction of poverty and social inequality for her citizens and hence is a story about poverty in the midst of plenty" (Mogalakwe and Nyamnjoh 2017: 6). This is particularly true for women.

In this book, I will focus on gender inequalities rooted in the country's patriarchal traditional culture, underpinned by patriarchal political structures and patriarchal religious institutions, which are markedly Christianized. Together, these have resulted in a breeding ground for rape culture and, consequently, in GBV. I will demonstrate how gender inequality in Botswana has a long and dreadful history. I will illustrate this next by sampling some demeaning Setswana proverbs about women, which are considered indigenous wisdom, and which distil and disclose widespread and culturally legitimated attitudes. This is also intended to acquaint the reader with just how damaging the culture is regarding attitudes to women—a situation that is partly responsible for the current GBV pandemic in Botswana.

"A Woman Is [Like] a Baboon"

Next, I will highlight some tendencies of traditional Setswana culture with reference to select gendered proverbs. This might begin to explain how Setswana culture has come to dovetail so well with certain biblical gendered tendencies. Taken together, I will argue, this alliance of patriarchal and gendered denigrations of women and girls has contributed to the powder keg of GBV we see in today's Botswana. I will go on to show that different selections from indigenous and biblical cultures can also effect help and healing.

Traditionally, that is, prior to the introduction of Christianity by missionaries who accompanied the colonizers, Batswana practiced highly accentuated gender roles assigned to each of women and men. That is, there has always been a strong and binary hierarchical demarcation of gender roles. Alongside gender, age also determines hierarchy. According to James Denbow and Phenyo Thebe (2006: 135) women were traditionally tasked with building, tilling of the soil, and making pots, baskets, and other household utensils. Robert Moffat, one of the earliest missionaries to Botswana, observed that Batswana women, in addition to rearing children, were "constantly employed; and during the season of picking and sowing their gardens, their task is galling, living on a course, scanty fare, and frequently having a baby fostered on their backs while they cultivate the ground" (Moffat 1842 cited by Nkomazana 2008, 3).

Men were tasked with roles that gave them power over women: As heads of households, as well as in community administration, including as chiefs.

Other than that, their more demanding roles included hunting, going to war, watching cattle, milking cows, and making mantles out of animal skins (Ibid).

These gendered roles were evaluated differently, with more importance and more status assigned to "male" than to "female" tasks. By extension, males were accorded more dignity. A traditional Setswana proverb says, *mosadi tshwene o jewa mabogo*, which literally translates as, "a woman is [like] a baboon worth only the deeds of her hands." This proverb is still very much alive in our culture and clearly devalues a woman's worth, which is measured entirely in terms of her service or deeds.

At traditional wedding ceremonies, meanwhile, and especially during the *go laya*, meaning "the advice ritual," which is one of the many rituals associated with Setswana marriage, the proverb is reiterated to the bride. No wonder that in her analysis of the advice ritual, Sibongile Ellece (2011) maintains that it is a time when other married women not only welcome but also initiate the bride into being a fool like themselves. During this ritual, which takes place prior to the giving of a bride to her in-laws, her gathered-together married female relatives take turns in giving her advice on how to become "a good wife" (Ellece 2011). Unfortunately, the advice is centered entirely on a woman's subordination in relation to her husband. Based on cultural expectations and orientations and on their own internalized experiences, the married women who take part in this advice ritual impress upon the new bride to take up and accept her submission, indeed, her servant-like position, and to serve and please her husband. She is told to work hard to ensure that her husband is happy, by cooking for him, cleaning for and cleaning up after him, and sexually availing herself at her husband's command. She is told to keep silent about any misgivings about her husband, including and/especially concerning his infidelities. In Setswana culture, it is commonly accepted that a man can be, indeed is expected to be, unfaithful to his wife, while such behavior is not tolerated from women (Kebaneilwe 2011).

This cultural attitude is also expressed in many traditional Setswana proverbs. One example is, *monna selepe wa fapanelwa*, meaning, "a man is [like] an axe, he is passed/swapped around." The functional meaning of this is that a man is strong, aggressive, and powerful, as well as justified in having multiple sexual partners, or to be simultaneously involved with several women; this, moreover, does not bring about condemnation or disapproval. Much like the proverb that says that *monna thotse waa nama*, meaning that a man is [like] a creeping plant that spreads all over the place and is hard to contain. Again, men's sexual (*creepy!*) behaviors are accommodated and justified. Indeed, the culture allows latitude for promiscuity for men but shuns it for women (Dube 2003; Kebaneilwe 2011). These attitudes have had profound consequences for women, including heightened vulnerability to all forms of discrimination, deprivation, abuse, violence, as well as to HIV infection and death. For instance, research shows that the HIV and AIDS pandemic, which had Botswana at its epicenter, affected more women than men both in terms of infection rates and with the additional burdens of caring for the orphaned, sick, and dying (Dube 2003).

Today, with widespread industrialization, modernization, and urbanization, a lot have changed. Setswana traditions, too, have adapted. Today both women and men have access to education; both can pursue professional careers after attaining education. But women are still expected to conform to traditional values in many ways and settings. Women still tend to come home after work and pick up the bulk of domestic and caregiving chores. Such chores include cleaning the house, cooking, and attending to children; meanwhile, many Batswana men come home from work and expect to rest, watch television, or read the newspaper. Therefore, in the present, as in the past, women remain burdened by social expectations and by the multiple roles that keep them disadvantaged.

Households were and still are important because they form the basic unit of social and political structures that are centered on the *kgotla:* The community gathering place and location where cases are heard and customary law is determined (Denbow and Thebe 2006, 135). The *kgotla,* too, was, for the longest time, the preserve of Batswana men—which leads us to another Setswana custom, whereby leadership positions are reserved for men, while women are moved to the peripheries. Again, traditional proverbs capture this clearly.

"Women Are [Like] Cows and Cannot Lead"

A Setswana proverb says, *ga di nke di etelelwa pele ke manamagadi,* literally "cows cannot lead the herd." The functional meaning is that there is something essential to or inherent in women that makes them ill-suited to leadership. The proverb advises that women follow or stay at the periphery of society. The effect of such a mindset is that women are barred or excluded from positions of authority, both in private and in public spaces. It also legitimates that power be in the hands of men.

The year 2003, however, witnessed the making of history, with the coronation of the first Motswana woman as paramount chief; Namely, Kgosi ("chief") Mosadi Seboko. [7] Kgosi Seboko's ultimate claim to her rightful position as paramount chief by birth-right, was not unopposed. Even though she is the first-born child of Kgosi Seboko I of the BaLete tribe of Ramotswa in the southeast of Botswana, for many of her own tribespeople, the idea of a woman chief was unthinkable. And yet, she took the office of the highest traditional, cultural and political space, hearing, and adjudicating cases.

Yet the *kgotla* none the less remains a predominantly male space, as is all too clear in the low number of women in the *Ntlo ya Dikgosi* ("House of Chiefs").[8] This institution is an advisory body to the National Assembly of Parliament on issues of national interest following the Constitution of Botswana.[9] Out of the 35 members of the *Ntlo ya Dikgosi,* women consistently make up less than 10%, with one report showing that in 2019, there was only one woman elected to the institution.[10] This indicates that the *bogosi* ("chieftaincy") continues to be a male preserve; indeed, in the prevailing patriarchal traditional mindset, women continue to be "cows."

The same tendency is visible in the parliament of the Republic of Botswana with only 11% of seats in the National Assembly held by women (i.e., 7 out of 63).[11] It is safe to conclude that in Botswana women's representation and participation in politics is lagging. While women have *legal access* to education and work, including in political settings, women's *representation* in places of leadership remains negligible. The traditional attitudes reflected in proverbs still hold sway, keeping women in subordinate positions. The strong cultural belief that *mosadi, mosalagae*, another Setswana proverb meaning "a woman's place is in the home," perpetuates and enforces the underrepresentation of women in leadership and decision-making positions (Cailleba and Kumar 2010, 333). Sadly, the attitudes are very much alive in present-day Botswana.

At every stage of their lives, women in Botswana tend to fall under the authority of males (Denbow and Thebe 2006, 135). Batswana women were, and still are, considered socially inferior to men and effectively regarded as minors even in full adulthood (Seng 1992). Traditionally, before marriage, a woman is under the authority of her father (or her brothers, in the absence of a father); after marriage she is regulated by her husband; and if she is widowed, her sons or her brothers take over as her guardians.

In contemporary Botswana, such traditional gender hierarchies and attitudes have been challenged by human rights and civil rights movements as well as by gender activists. There have been policy changes to address gender disparities, but in terms of practice on the ground, change is slow in coming. I will discuss some policy and legal changes shortly. The point I want to bring home is that the attitudes of the proverbs, depicting women as baboons and cows, not fit for public leadership, and subordinated to males, persist unabated in Botswana. Sadly, such demeaning attitudes to women come not only from men but also from women. As I will demonstrate later in this book, patriarchy is a systemic monster, and its insidious power transpires not only in the horrors of physical rape of women but also in the raping of mindsets as well. No one living in a rape culture is immune to its effects and not only men but also women internalize its toxic influence.

In addition to the examples of demeaning Setswana proverbs about women, it is also necessary to show that there are a few positive proverbs about women which sit side by side with the negative ones. For instance, *mosadi ke thari ya sechaba* is an ambiguous proverb that means two things: Namely, that "a woman is the placenta of the nation" and that "a woman is a carrier of the nation" (Ellece 2011). Hence, in the Setswana language, *thari* is both a placenta and a carrier, with the latter referring to a specially curved piece of animal skin traditionally used by women to carry children on their backs (Ellece 2011). Using the *thari* to fasten the child firmly on its mother's back ensured the child's security as the mother walked long distances to fetch wood, water, or look after the family's domestic animals (Nkomazana 2008, 86). Both the above meanings do not detract from Setswana culture being patriarchal, but the proverb also recognizes an underlying fear or acknowledgment of the mysterious power and peculiar strength associated with womanhood or motherhood.

There is an apparent contradiction in the above-cited proverbs' perception and presentation of woman as both "nothing" and "everything." Perhaps this is not surprising, given the irony that, metaphorically speaking, as Newsom puts it, woman is the social fabric of patriarchy, the essential thread that joins the pieces but, equally, indicates the seams where the fabric is subject to tears (Newsom 1989, 155). This explains the contradiction in Setswana culture and proverbs that represent a woman as *both* essential for the existence of society (as the "placenta of the nation") while also belittling her (as nothing but a baboon or cow). She is celebrated as essential but as not able to lead. The positive comes with imposed restriction and is therefore, ultimately, not helpful for addressing gendered inequalities.

The Socio-political and Cultural Landscape of Botswana: Past and Present

Botswana operates under a dual legal system, which combines what is variously called indigenous, customary, or traditional law with the received law, or Roman-Dutch and English law, also known as "common law," inherited from former colonial rule (Cailleba and Kumar 2010; Swartz et.al., 2015, 12). The Constitution, which represents common law, gives latitude and prominence to customary law on a range of matters, and this flexibility has significant implications for women's rights and is more fully noted by Cailleba and Kumar (2010). Customary law is largely unwritten and is deeply rooted in Setswana culture and traditions. In regulating day-to-day life, it continues to take precedence over what might be regarded as the modernizing influence of common law. This situation is especially debilitating for women, as they barely have what might be regarded as "rights" in the context of Botswana's traditional mores and laws. In most cases, administrators, and executors of customary law, which include community chiefs and advisers, are men—moreover, men who uphold the traditions and status quo that serve and promote their interests (Maundeni 2002; Schapera 1966). Customary law does not acknowledge women's rights in common law and has, consequently, continued the patriarchal legacy of inequality between men and women and promoted the stereotypical perceptions about women and their roles in society, conveyed aptly and aphoristically in traditional proverbs. Therefore, the current dual legal system has not served women's rights and representation well (Cailleba and Kumar, 2010, 331).

12 A Contextual Background

While the Botswana government has taken significant steps towards ensuring basic human rights, including protection concerning gender, ever since independence in 1966 setting in place and qualifying important protections and laws, this has *not* always translated into enactment and lived realities. (I will give an example below.) But first, although it is not the primary focus of this book, it is important to mention strides in Botswana in terms of legal protection for persons of homosexual orientation. In 2019, Botswana made a landmark ruling in the case involving Lesbians, Gays & Bisexuals of Botswana LEGABIBO[12] versus The Attorney General, in which the Hight Court of Botswana ruled in favor of LEGABIBO's representative Letsweletse Motshidiemans, arguing the criminalization of anal intercourse between consenting adults violates the fundamental rights of gay persons (Lekgowe 2023, 1). Less than five years later, the decision is being challenged, this time by the Church under its wing of the Evangelical Fellowship Botswana (EFB), an umbrella body comprising several churches leading anti-gay public demonstrations.[13] Regrettably, the same government of Botswana bowed to church pressure in a case in which the parliament was to interrogate a Bill to give same-sex loving people more rights and freedoms. In another online report, it is stated as follows:

> A fortnight ago, members of the Evangelical Fellowship Botswana made public demonstrations and marched against decriminalizing same-sex relations, and their efforts paid dividends. The object of the Bill is to amend Section 164(a) and (c) of the Penal Code (CAP. 08:01), which criminalizes "carnal knowledge between two adults against the order of nature." Section 164 (a) and (c) was declared unconstitutional in the case of the Attorney General and Letsweletse Motshidiemang, Court of Appeal's No. CACGB- 157-19 …. Even though this was a landmark victory for the LGBTIQ+ community, a draft of the above Bill, which was intended to be presented to the National assembly would open floodgates of immorality as it seeks to legalise homosexuality, according to the EFB.
>
> (Kapeng, 2023)[14]

From the above report, it is clear that what might be called progressive laws have not always translated into equally progressive attitudes on the ground. Furthermore, by bowing to the church's pressure and suspending the case, the government of Botswana has demonstrated its reluctance and lack of political will to address the marginalization and discrimination of minority groups, in this case Lesbian, Gay, Bisexual, Transgender, Intersex and Queer persons (LGBTIQ+). It is perhaps no surprise, therefore, that with gender inequality pertaining to women, too, not enough progress is being made. Moreover, as I shall show, religious actors again play a part in this obstruction of progress. Hence, despite efforts by the government and pressure from activist groups to curb gender inequality, GBV and other forms of gender injustice prevail.

Let me now discuss a few laws that, while commendable, show up glaring gaps yet to be filled. Hence, there is a gulf between Botswana's laws and how the country is widely perceived by outsiders (i.e., as stable, peaceful, and prosperous), on the one hand, and, on the other, the sexist and damaging realities on the ground, which are harming particularly Batswana women and girls who remain at the margins of leadership and most vulnerable to GBV. Worth noting is that at the time of writing this book (2022), the Botswana Constitution is undergoing revision. Changes and refinement in law, including constitutional law, are welcome, but this is not the end of the matter. Advances in actual change must involve efforts on multiple fronts, including—as will become the book's focus—in the realms of religious life, given that in Botswana religion is all-pervasive. Indigenous and Christian religions are powerful and inter-twined forces in day-to-day life in Botswana, and their influence must no longer be underestimated.

Protection from Discrimination Based on Gender

The Botswana Constitution's Section 15 (3) prohibits discrimination based on gender, but there is no compulsion for individuals, in private or much of public life to comply (Cailleba and Kumar 2010, 331). As a result of the inadequacy of enforcing this law, women continue to be discriminated against. In its severest manifestations, this is clear in rates of domestic violence (DV) and abuse, as well as the sharp rise in so-called passion killings (a notorious term for homicide), both of which are shockingly skewed in terms of gender, with women far more likely to be victims than men. For instance, the Sunday Standard newspaper reported that in 747 cases of passion killings committed in 2003, 689 were females.[15] During the same period (2003–2012), rape cases, DV, defilement of girls, and physical assault were all reported to have increased. For example, rape cases rose from 1,506 in 2003 to 2,073 in 2012, while homicide cases resulting from intimate partner violence (IPV) increased from 54 in 2003 to 89 in 2012.[16] In 2018, the numbers had gone up to 194 murder cases, in which 87 were female victims of IPV (Kgosikebatho 2018).

I know from my personal experience as a woman and as a mother with adult daughters that when a woman reports an incidence of abuse by an intimate male partner, she is liable to being perceived as "a bad woman" who wants to destroy a man by getting him in trouble with the police. The very police system that is by common law expected to protect citizens can be part of the problem. The kind of comments I have encountered include, "you women are evil. After using a man and exploiting him financially, you now want him to go to prison." I have heard such remarks on more than one occasion at different police stations when reporting GBV. Despite the existence of a protective law, discrimination based on gender continues to exert its grip. The law is ineffectual and those tasked with enforcing it do not always have the training, as in my case, to respond sensitively or effectively to GBV, or even to refrain from derogatory comments. Instead, more prominent, yet again, is the kind of stereotype that regards women with suspicion, as evil tricksters, such as is captured in the Setswana proverb, *o se bone tholwana borethe, teng ga yone goa baba,* meaning, "a woman's good looks are nothing but a cover for the evil inside her."

Domestic Violence Act (2008)

The DV Act was passed in 2008 and criminalizes many forms of violence that are, once more, disproportionately inflicted by men against women. However, because it operates in parallel and simultaneously with customary law, which tends to side-line or outright ignore women's rights, criminalization of DV is often in effect nullified in Botswana (Swartz et.al. 2015, 12). Possibly as a direct result, reports show that many women are reluctant to report DV. Several factors are blamed for this reluctance, including lack of services, lack of protection, social stigma, and women's perceived strength to endure hardships and violence especially from their intimate male partners and the admiration accorded to this silent endurance (Maundeni 2002, 266). Still, another factor that contributes to women victims of GBV's reluctance to report is the lack of shelters where such victims may be kept safe. I discuss this below.

As noted above, the police service in Botswana, often tasked with handling reports as first responders to DV, is not always either trained or even willing to act on behalf of victims, instead referring victims to seek advice from their relatives. This was certainly my own experience. Such trivialization of DV has led women to lose hope in the courts and the police and to opt for silence and repression (Swartz et.al. 2015). Moreover, while there is evidence that men too experience GBV, men reporting DV are prone to being mocked for being deficiently masculine, making reports by men against women even less likely than disclosures of violence made by women against male perpetrators. As indicated in one study, men are ashamed to report abuse and violence perpetrated against them by women because they get derogatory comments like, "You are a man how can you report such a thing? You are a coward … lazy or useless" (Petrina 2023, 38). However, for the purpose of this book, I will restrict my focus to GBV against women, the group disproportionately affected by GBV, including IPV, and partner homicide (see Grace 2021; Machisa and Dorp 2012 *passim*).[17]

Another inadequacy of the DV Act of Botswana is that while it empowers the police to remove victims from their homes, it does not provide places where they can go for safeguarding. There are three shelters, all of which are run by non-governmental organizations. These are the Kagisano Women's Shelters for abused women (Grace 2021, 409). The shelters were founded by Kagisano Society, which is an organization that is said to have been offering humanitarian services in Botswana since the 1970s, when Botswana was receiving many asylum seekers fleeing unrest from liberation wars in neighboring countries.[18] Since the reduction of refugees coming into the country in the 1990s, the organization shifted its focus to addressing GBV, which was by now escalating in the country. This led to the establishment of the first women's shelter in the country, which was opened in 1998.[19] Currently, the Kagisano Society offers counseling, community outreach, and education as well as limited emergency and temporary accommodation to those fleeing from GBV. This provision is, however, limited to the capital city, Gaborone, which is located near the southern border with South Africa, on the edge of Botswana's vastness. Hence, the shelter is not only inadequate for meeting the demands for safely housing the numerous victims of DV but it is also inaccessible to much of the population (Swartz et.al. 2015, 14). After all, the shelter is not even enough to service Gaborone itself, which according to the latest Botswana Population Census has a population of 246,325, around a tenth of the country's total population of 2,359,602 (Statistics Botswana 2022). In a country where GBV is currently the highest in world at 92.93 per 100, 000 people according to the World Population Review (2023), a lot more needs to be done to address the need for more shelters alongside other resources to assist victims and survivors of GBV.

The other woman-centered association in Botswana is Emang Basadi, which literally means "women must stand up!" Established in 1986 by a group of concerned citizens, the association serves women by raising awareness of discrimination against them through lobbying, advocacy, and capacity building. It also provides legal assistance and counseling aimed at empowering women.[20] "Its catalyst was the enactment of the 1982 Citizenship Act, which sought to deny women married to non-citizen men the right to pass their citizenship to their offspring" (Selolwane 2004). Agitating for reform and calling out the laws of the country brought Emang Basadi much criticism from a society where authority by men was and is revered as the accepted norm. However, the association was not distracted by the accusations that it was led by a group of "misguided, Western-educated young women out of touch with their African reality and therefore unrepresentative of African womanhood" (Selolwane 2004, 2). Today Emang Basadi struggles to survive because of lack of funding and is reliant on foreign aid. As observed by Obagboye Grace (2021), there is, ultimately, a lack of political will to address issues related to GBV in Botswana, as perhaps is also the case in other African countries.[21]

This is further entrenched by the cultural norm that expects women to persevere "valiantly" in their marriages, suffering in silence, and turns a blind eye to husbands who beat their wives (Maundeni 2002). Therefore, women often stay in abusive relationships, whether they are married or not, often for a complex web of reasons including the abovementioned ones, which show up a lack of viable alternatives. According to Tapologo Maundeni, a Motswana female Professor of Social Work, less educated women tend to stay longer in abusive marriages than more educated women who may have some degree of economic independence as well as more knowledge of support services (Maundeni 2002, 266). Some women, indeed, stay because of economic

16   A Contextual Background

dependency on their abusers, others because they are told that abuse is inevitable, and others again, because there is nowhere else to go (Ibid). Other culturally infused factors include the shame and stigma associated with separation and divorce or not "having a man." A divorced woman is sometimes treated with contempt and suspicion and carries blame for a marriage breakup, which, in turn, curtails her prospects for re-marriage. For these reasons and more, many women in Botswana have opted for silence and resignation, and many have died at the hands of cruel husbands or intimate partners (Kebaneilwe 2011, 282). The issues touched on here will be explored further in the subsequent chapters in this book. Let me continue with detailing more of the legal protections in Botswana—and with their inadequacy in terms of the discrepancy between law and its lack of implementation.

The Botswana Penal Code Amendment

Patrice Cailleb and Rhekha Kumar (2010, 332–3) discuss how the Penal Code of Botswana was amended in 1998 to include "a gender sensitive definition of rape." This amendment means that rape is acknowledged and outlawed as a serious crime, and yet, to date, spousal rape is still not included in or recognized in law (Cailleb and Kumar, 2010: 333). Any assertion of gender sensitivity in the rape law can be further seen to be deficient in that not only marital rape goes unmentioned but so does rape of a man by a man. The assumption, instead, is that rape refers to men's rape of women only. Furthermore, the law has contributed to turning marriage into a risky institution where the right of a woman, once married, to refuse sex, including unprotected sex, with her husband is compromised. Now, because married women cannot report rape by their husbands, many have been exposed not only to violence and rape but also, given the region's high rates of HIV, to infection with the virus, which, particularly before wide dispersal of antiretroviral drugs, was often a prelude to Aids and, often, to premature and drawn-out death. Nowadays, rape victims have access to preventative prophylaxes, but married women tend not to request them because sex with their husbands is not classified as rape—even when they are unwilling or when sex has taken place without informed consent concerning exposure to risk of HIV (or other STD) infection. Again, this has much to do with the traditional belief that a woman is subject to her husband and her existence and purpose are to please him, including through sexual gratification, and even if this is against her will—namely, rape. This will be explored further shortly.

The Sexual Harassment Act

Sexual harassment by a public officer is considered a crime,[22] but there is no provision if the crime is committed outside of the domain of public service and, as mentioned earlier, sexual harassment, especially targeting women and girls, happens everywhere and often very publicly. Why is there no provision in the law to criminalize and prosecute such incidences? The narrowly framed law shows, first, reluctance on the part of legislators to address the issue of sexual harassment, and, second, that sexual harassment is not considered all that serious. The effect is to make women and girls in Botswana vulnerable to behavior that ranges from microaggressions to threatening behavior and serious, frightening, and damaging misconduct. This, in turn, serves to legitimate rape culture. While it may be the case that law often represents an ideal, capturing something that is far from being realized—as in the example of Botswana's Constitution legislating against gender inequality—and while laws cannot cover all eventualities and scenarios, it is very worrisome that harassment committed openly against women and girls, inclusive of sexual harassment, is almost entirely ignored by lawmakers.

The Abolition of Marital Power Act (2004)

The Abolition of Marital Power Act of 2004 gives equal power to both partners in marriage by common law (Cailleb and Kumar, 2010: 336). This Act was introduced to recognize married women's rights to family/marital property in terms of ownership and management (Maundeni 2016). Prior to this, a married woman had no legal right to marital property and even if she contributed financially to such property, it was under the sole ownership of her husband. Married women were regarded as minors and needed the consent of their husbands to carry out any transactions. Meanwhile, their husbands had property rights over all matrimonial assets (Cailleb and Kumar, 2010; see also, Quansah 2005, 5). Until 2004, a husband could sell the marital home without his wife's knowledge or consent, and she had no say over decisions, even if they directly affected her. As a result, women were sometimes left homeless or impoverished, without information or agency to intervene.

 I recall here the painful narrative of one woman who was a well-educated professional working in Botswana's foreign ministry. She told me her sad story of how, during her marriage in the 1980s, she was sent to study in the United Kingdom, leaving her husband and children back home. She returned to Botswana, following two years of study, to find new tenants in what used to be her marital home, a home to which she had contributed considerably. It was upon ringing the bell at the gate that she learned how her husband had sold the house and property. She engaged her lawyers who failed dismally in getting the property restored to her or even obtaining some compensation. The reason was that the legal system provided no protection for women like her. Her husband was not guilty of any crime as she had no legal right to the property or to any proceeds deriving from it. She left the court and her marriage empty-handed to start again.

 Another sad narrative concerns a woman, now in her early 70s, whom I first encountered in 2014. She is a retired social worker, and we met when

I moved to my newly mortgaged property after leaving my own ten-year marriage empty-handed. We started sharing our life stories, and I told her how I lost everything I had worked for during my marriage and how this was why I had just taken on a large mortgage of the residential property adjacent to hers. She then narrated how she had suffered in an abusive marriage where her now-late ex-husband would emotionally and physically abuse her when drunk. She went on to tell me how one day, she and her two daughters got evicted from a house she had owned with her husband. At that time, they were still married, and the husband had decided to sell their house, without her knowing this. Ultimately, she was left on the street with her daughters and had to find refuge back at her parents' place in a rural area. For her, that was the breaking point that led her to get a divorce and, as was the norm, she went away with nothing, picking up the pieces and raising her two daughters by herself.

So, has the Abolition of Marital Power Act empowered women as equal partners in marriage, ownership, and management of the marital property? In my assessment, despite the existence of the Act, many women still find themselves robbed of their marital or matrimonial assets. That is, men still find a way to manipulate the porous patriarchal system which makes it easier for them than for women to execute control over matrimonial property. From my personal experience, the questioning and screening at government offices do not favor women. Hence, while both men and women are required to provide proof of marital status, by showing either a marriage/divorce certificate or an affidavit to the contrary, men can more easily conceal their status and claim singlehood, while women, on account of a change of surname at marriage, cannot. Consequently, many men have still managed to dispose of shared marital property without their spouse's consent or knowledge because the system continues to favor them. This is exacerbated by the absence of a law that requires marrying couples to register both names on whatever assets they acquire during their union. From personal experience, men, citing tradition, prefer that assets are registered in their name only, as head of their households. This often passes easily because we Batswana women have been raised to be subordinates to our male partners, and such decisions go unchallenged. As I have already indicated earlier, even during marriage ceremonies and rituals, new brides are advised on self-sacrifice and subordination to their husbands. It is, therefore, not surprising that despite the existence of such acts as the Abolition of Marital Power Act, many women still become victims, losing economic assets. The Act was instituted to protect women in marriages, but its efficacy leaves something to be desired.

Sadder still, the practical reality is that customary law marriages (as opposed to common law marriages) are not part of the new Act. This means women in such marriages are subject to the authority of their husbands following traditional customs (Quansah 2005). Emmanuel Quansah observes that in both types of dual legislation—namely, common and customary law—the husband is recognized as the head of the family who exercises power and control over his wife and children (Quansah 2005, 12). Quansah further proposes that perhaps the reason why the Act excluded customary marriage law was in a bid to preserve patriarchal Setswana culture and tradition (Ibid). Like other attempts to undo oppressive cultural practices that deny women equal power and opportunities as men, amendment to marriage law has to this day been met with resistance from conservative mindsets that strive to maintain a status quo that favors men and heteronormativity.

In the last 56 years since Botswana attained independence from colonial rule, Batswana women have continued to endure subordinate status. In many ways, for all the new laws, women and girls are still widely sexualized and treated as commodities, and wives continue to be treated as part of their husband's belongings (Tabengwa and Fergus 1998). It remains acceptable for Batswana men to chastise their wives and children because Setswana culture allows latitude to do so (Maundeni 2002). While the country gained independence from colonial rule, women did not gain full independence. Their oppression, moreover, is exerted by members of their own people, which, in my view, makes it even more painful. Being oppressed by internal forces is in some ways more oppressive and more damaging than being oppressed by external forces. By this, I mean that being ruled, controlled, and regulated by colonial rulers gave us a common opponent; we stood together and collectively resisted this rule, culminating in the independence of our own country and standing in solidarity with other colonized countries. But being stifled by our own, our own men and boys, means as women and girls, we experience a very poignant kind of suffering and betrayal.

The Religious Landscape of Botswana: Spiritualization of Patriarchy

Botswana is home to many religious traditions, including multiple denominations of Christianity, African Indigenous Religions, and minor representations of Islam, Hinduism, and Bahá'í (Haron and Jensen 2008). According to the Botswana Population Census (2011), 79% of citizens are members of Christian groups, 15% espouse no religion, 4% are adherents of the *Badimo* indigenous religious group, and all other religious groups together constitute less than 2% of the population.

More than ten years on from the census, not much has changed in Botswana in terms of the religious landscape and demography, as the Report on International Religious Freedom: Botswana (2022) estimated in 2022 that 71.6% of the population are Christian, 27% are members of the indigenous religious groups (*Badimo*), and the rest are of other religions, with very minor representation (Islam, Buddhism, and Hinduism).[23] However, it is worth noting that what seems like wobbly statistics with reference to the percentages for indigenous religions, namely the 4% in 2011 and the 27% in 2022—noted above, is a reflection that not all who name themselves Christian admit to simultaneously practicing their indigenous beliefs as well. As a result, the 4% and or even the 27% are arguably much higher. As James Amanze observes, indigenous beliefs in Botswana are unabated despite the country being predominately Christian. The beliefs, as Amanze further argues, "give the people a sense of self-identity" (Amanze 2003, 43).

Nonetheless, Christianity is still by far Botswana's dominant religion in terms of the number of self-declared followers, and it exists alongside and sometimes entwined with indigenous religious traditions and they run deep (cf. Amanze 1994; Haron 2007, Nkomazana 2008). The first Christian missionary to settle in Botswana was David Livingstone in 1847, and the spread of Christianity was rapid (Haron and Jensen, 2008). The general trend, of note for my purposes, is that in multiple African contexts, African Traditional Religion and Christianity have worked together to oppress and marginalize women (Togarasei, 2013: 3). This is mainly because both sets of religions are predominantly patriarchal.

Indigenous, or African Traditional Religions of Botswana, much like indigenous political and cultural traditions, are explicitly patriarchal. The traditional Setswana religious belief in and veneration for ancestors or ancestral spirits, *Badimo* in Setswana, is predominantly to the memory of men. The belief is that when people die, they take up some new spiritual existence as *Badimo* (Dube, 1999). They transition into spiritual entities and, importantly, take up a more powerful existence than when they were alive, acting as intermediaries between *Modimo* (God) and the living. In effect, the ancestors are the living dead. Noteworthy is that *Modimo* is tacitly masculine in that, though the noun itself, *Modimo*—always used in the singular in Setswana, has no explicit gender, it is referred to in masculine terms as *Rra* "Sir/Mr" or *Rraetsho*, "our father." This is also true for the use of the noun *Badimo* (ancestors). Musa Dube maintains that the Setswana noun *Badimo*, which is always in the plural, has no assigned gender and that both women and men are eligible to join the community of *Badimo* after death (2001, 179–185). While that is true, we cannot escape the essentially patriarchal culture within which Setswana religiosity is embedded.

We have already seen, for instance, how in Setswana culture, both past and present, women mostly occupy marginal positions under the subordination of men, and I wonder how possible it is that when they transition into the spiritual realm of *Badimo* they now become equal with men. This is not to suggest the impossibility of this, but, as other scholars have argued, the ancestors or ancestral spirits were and are most often conceived of as male and even referred to as *Borramogolwane* "forefathers" (Nkomazana 2008, 84), never as foremothers. This suggests, if anything, that to become *Badimo* and part of the powerful spirit world, females lose their femaleness and become, essentially, promoted to male status. This is certainly what language usage implies. The idea that *Badimo* is a gender-neutral noun should not detract us from actual practice and actual treatment of women. There is, moreover, subtle gendering of the ancestors, which reimposes typical gendered hierarchies.

I agree completely with Dube that the introduction of Christianity and colonial culture reinforced and strengthened male domination in Setswana culture, not least, because British colonial culture itself was firmly patriarchal (Dube 2012, 336). Gendered discrimination was no new thing. The introduction of Christianity handed to Batswana a spiritual space that was firmly androcentric: The divinity of God the Father and Jesus the Son (Dube 2012). Alongside this, there is the more ambiguous Holy Spirit whose gender is hard to determine. In my view, the ambiguity and elusive presentation of the Holy Spirit play on a similar subtlety as the *Badimo* concept but again hides and affirms promotion of male gender. Both colonial and Setswana cultures reinforced patriarchal power structures and even ungendered power, such as of *Badimo* or the Holy Spirit do not change this significantly.

Such conceptualizations and perceptions not only marginalize women but also promote a spirituality of patriarchy by divinizing gender inequality to the detriment of women (Nkomazana, 2008, 84). The forefathers/ancestors are to this day highly significant in the Setswana religio-cultural worldview, as they are believed to be powerful in influencing the living, but yet again, they are constructed as predominantly male, thereby, once more, promoting the notion of male superiority (Nkomazana, 2008). The spiritual *Badimo* as ancestors are sacred beings who regulate society and ensure its stability; as noted by Dube, they are the thread that connects contemporary society with its past and maps its future (Dube 2012). But they also mimic the gender hierarchies of the past and present-day worlds. As people (more prominently men) of the past, the ancestors are not only memorialized but also kept active in present-day life through what is known as ancestor veneration (Amanze 2003). The Christian God and his son Jesus have some compatibility with traditional ideas and beliefs of divinity—God too is revered and in relationship with Jesus, just as *Modimo* and *Badimo* are in relationship, with all apparently ungendered but conceived of in predominantly male-gendered ways. No wonder the two religious traditions have since the coming of Christianity, co-existed largely in harmony in Botswana. The sad thing is that the two traditions have colluded against women who in both worlds exist on the peripheries, as the ones to be ruled, and subordinated.

Through their habitual marginalization, women, even in death, are still relegated to an inferior status; they are still comparatively invisible and voiceless, while their male counterparts, again, gain powers to rule, direct, speak, and control, even from beyond the grave. This is true in Botswana's traditional religious belief in ancestors and is reinforced by Christianity, with Jesus, too, being male and also ruling from beyond the grave (Matthew 28:6; Mark 15:42–47). A point noted by Fidelis Nkomazana is that Setswana patriarchal culture constructs male leadership as natural and eternal (Nkomazana 2008, 29), which finds echoes and counterparts in biblical texts. Therefore, the

Bible presents a Motswana Christian with a world not so unfamiliar to them and hence, as noted already, it is not altogether surprising that around a third of the population of Batswana subscribe to Christianity while also maintaining their traditional religious beliefs.

It is not an exaggeration to conclude that in Botswana Christianity entered a world already entrenched with gender inequality and made an easy home there. Gender inequality in Botswana is manifest in socio-economic, socio-cultural, and religio-political spaces. In pre-colonial Botswana, I argue, as maintained by indigenous, including indigenous religious, beliefs, and practices, women were disadvantaged in comparison with men: They carried a greater burden of day-to-day work, which was considered less prestigious than men's work; they had less status and authority, did not rise to leadership roles, and were poorer and more vulnerable to all kinds of oppression. Christianity, with its own gendered hierarchies, landed on fertile soil in Botswana. The next question, then, is what impact did Christianity have in terms of the prevailing status quo of gender inequality already in pre-missionary Botswana? In some ways, I will argue, there is continuity rather than only disruption.

Batswana women and men, whether they subscribe to indigenous traditions or to prevailing Christian norms, tend to be socialized in different and unequal ways. Men are treated as superiors, both as leaders of their households and as the ones who dominate in the public domains, as political, institutional, and religious leaders. Women's thankless labor to support their households and nurture and feed their families goes largely unnoticed and unrewarded. The missionaries who brought Christianity to Botswana did not do anything to change the gendered status quo—not least, probably, because they were importing inequalities from their own contexts (Nkomazana 2008, 2). In my view, this action on the part missionaries was further legitimated through use of the Bible. As the sacred text at the center of the Christian faith, the missionaries ushered in yet more narratives of predominantly male protagonists, narratives where women's stories tend to be scant or omitted (Kebaneilwe and Ellece 2020,44). Therefore, the Bible only added more to what was already on the ground in terms of gender inequality. It also explains why the Bible and the Christian faith found a congenial home in Botswana as is evidenced by the large Christian following in the population. Hence, the missionaries, even though they (like Livingstone, quoted above) noted some inequalities, continued to perpetuate male dominance and used the Bible in this endeavor (Nkomazana, 2008). Interestingly, the contribution of women in the early days of Christianity in Botswana (whether as missionaries or converts) is not at all well documented in missionary literature, which instead concentrates predominantly on male players, often referred to as the "natives" (Tlou 1985). The resonance between Setswana traditional religious beliefs and Christianity where gender is concerned is pronounced. With both, the inclination has been to promote ideas of male superiority and dominance, and female subservice and marginality.

A Contextual Background   23

Sadly, while African women generally make up the greater part of church congregations, they continue in large part to remain voiceless and invisible—just as they were unvoiced and omitted in church life histories (Robert 2014, 117). Studying specifically Pentecostal churches in Botswana, Rosinah Gabaitse (2017) reiterates that the patriarchal context of churches denies women prominence and leadership, which would see them move from the margins. She engages with one biblical text that has implications for freedom from oppression:

> The spirit of the Lord is on me because he has anointed me to proclaim good news to the poor. He has sent me to proclaim freedom for the prisoners and recovery of sight for the blind, to set the oppressed free, to proclaim the year of the Lord's favour.
>
> (Luke 4:18–19)

Gabaitse (2017) argues that these verses are spiritualized to emphasize the eschatological message regarding the saving of the soul while minimizing what the same could mean in the social world. That is, Pentecostal churches tend to focus on and interpret the above text to mean spiritual blindness, spiritual poverty, and spiritual oppression and overlook actual, physical, real flesh-and-blood issues of poverty, oppression (especially oppression of women by men), or what it could mean for people living with a disability. As Gabaitse further explains, Pentecostal churches in Botswana and surrounding countries like Zimbabwe and South Africa teach and reinforce male supremacy and female subordination with legislative force. This, she argues, includes patriarchal interpretations of other texts like Ephesians 5 (vv. 22–24) which are interpreted to support male prestige and women's submission (Gabaitse 2017, 61).

In summary, spiritualizing texts, as is widely done in Pentecostal churches, only serves to spiritualize gender inequality and make it appear like a natural, God-given situation. In a text like Luke 4:18–19 cited above, I would argue that spiritualizing its interpretation, as noted by Gabaitse, further serves to avoid interpretations that would disturb the status quo of male domination over and marginalization of females and other vulnerable groups (including the poor and those living with disability). The point is that if texts such as the example given here were read and interpreted to address physical, sociopolitical, and economic issues, women's current predicament of inequality, marginalization, and oppression could be effectively addressed and this could yield significant improvement in terms of gender disparity (Gabaitse 2017, 60–61). Hence, Luke 4:18–19 "… to set the oppressed free …" could be read to mean that oppression of any kind is not a good thing, and in the case of male-female relations. it could mean gender inequality should be dealt with to procure women's freedom from oppression by men. Such an interpretation would be a gender-sensitive one and would have the potential to nurture the seeds of gender equality between men and women. However, because such a reading would upset the status quo of male supremacy and female subordination in Botswana, it is avoided, ignored, and not entertained, especially by church authorities that are predominantly male.

Christianity has continued to influence patriarchal perceptions of women and men because as already indicated, the biblical text is androcentric and applied to this purpose. Concerning the creation account of Genesis 2:4ff. and the Pauline teaching on the headship of men in Ephesians 5:22, Lovemore Togarasei maintains that the two texts have served to promote dangerous models of masculinity (Togarasei 2013, 3).[24] The headship of Christ over the Church is translated to affirm the headship of husbands over their wives. Such translations or interpretations tend to award men unchallenged authority over women, especially in already patriarchal contexts like Botswana where headship is equated with maleness, power, and domination over vulnerable others. Interpretations of scripture, like the ones given here, have allowed even those men who are not "Christ-like" leaders or providers for their families, the entitlement to lord over their wives (Togarasei 2013, 3). The result has not been favorable for those deemed weak and subservient, especially for women and girls.

In Botswana, such biblical views and interpretations of biblical texts regularly condone and support Botswana's traditional culture that subordinates women to men (and vice versa). Batswana women have nowhere to run, as the church is saturated with beliefs and practices similarly damaging in terms of gender injustice as those of wider society. This has seen Batswana women further pushed to the peripheries in private and in public life, especially away from positions of authority, leadership, and decision-making. These ideas and more will be discussed more fully in the next chapters.

Conclusion

In this chapter, I have discussed several issues that point to the collusion between indigenous culture and Christianity in Botswana, which have transpired in the oppression of women and girls. My southern African nation state, regionally and internationally lauded for its democracy, low levels of corruption, and impressive economic growth, is also characterized by gender inequality and very high rates of GBV, disproportionately targeted at women and girls. Traditionally, women in Botswana do not have equal rights; they are often not even regarded as autonomous persons, such as in regard to property rights within marriage. Women have been and are treated as commodities. As children, girls are under the guardianship and protection of their fathers, their brothers, or other male relatives, and after marriage, they fall under the authority and control of their husbands. Gender roles were and continue to be clearly demarcated, and women perform the lowly rated caregiving roles, as well as cooking, cleaning, and tilling the earth to produce food for their households. Men were and are assigned more dominant, authoritative, and prestigious roles, as heads of their households, chiefs, or community leaders, as well as hunters and tenders of cows (with cows constituting a high-prestige creature and commodity in Setswana culture). Much of the hard labor allocated to men tends to be seasonal, while women's assigned duties were and are continuous, throughout the year. This reliance on women to do the day-to-day chores without respite has continued into modern and urban life where, alongside participation in professional life, women are still expected to do all, or at least the bulk of, household chores and caregiving.

Christianity was introduced to Botswana as part of colonization, and it did not bring improvement in terms of raising women's status. Unequal power relations between men and women have continued to define gender relations in Botswana. Notably, colonization and Christianization have left the country with an inherited Roman-Dutch law and English law, collectively branded common law. This legal system continues to operate concurrently with traditional customary law. Since Botswana's independence in 1966, the hybrid system has seen the introduction of and some significant amendments to the Constitution and penal code. The changes are aimed at mitigating gender inequality and improving women's rights. However, in practical terms, the efficacy of changes is hardly discernible. This is due to strong resistance emanating from traditionally held customs and beliefs that have continued to shape attitudes and mindsets from generation to generation, coupled with the prominence given to customary law over common law. Together with Christianity, indigenous traditional cultures and religions of Botswana have maintained women's oppression and subordination under male supremacy, which, as we shall see in the ensuing chapters of this book, have led to the escalation of GBV in my country.

Notes

1 *CIA World Fact Book*, 2022. 'Religions: Botswana.'
2 'Motswana' refers to a citizen of Botswana; the plural is 'Batswana.' The native language and the culture of Botswana are both called 'Setswana.' However, 'Tswana' is the colonial term used to refer to the people, their language, *and* their culture. In this book, I prefer the native terms.
3 According to the UN Women: Global Database on Violence Against Women-Botswana (1998), "in Botswana, 3 in 5 women have been victims of assault, sexual harassment, sexual exploitation, severe beating, rape, incest, socio-economic abuse, murder, or verbal and emotional abuse."
4 Botswana is widely celebrated as an economic success story on the African continent. Botswana is not unaffected by the wider region's poverty, civil unrest, and wars. I will go on to revisit some of these matters below.
5 *The Conversation*, 29 November 2022.
6 Worldometer, 2023. 'Botswana Population,' (live), 26 September 2023.
7 Contributor, 2003. *Pambazuka News*, 'Botswana: First Female Paramount Chief welcomed,' 4 September 2003.
8 Parliament of Botswana, 'About *Ntlo ya Dikgosi.*'
9 Ibid.
10 *Sunday Standard Reporter*, 2019. 'Only one Woman Elected to *Ntlo ya Dikgosi*,' 18 November 2019.

11 Pini Botlhoko, 2022. 'Johannesburg: Women's Underrepresentation in Politics in Botswana, 14 March 2022.
12 LEGABIBO stands for 'Lesbiana, Gays & Bisexauls Botswana.' LEGABIBO was initiated in 1998 and is a Botswana human rights group who advocates particularly for the legal and social rights for members of Botswana's LGBTQ+ communities. Much of the continent of Africa has laws in place that discriminate harshly against homosexual acts and orientation. Botswana has followed South Africa and Cape Verde in decriminalizing consensual homosexual sex acts. As with the advancement of other rights pertaining to gender, the Bible has proved to be a tool of liberation, but more often a tool of obstruction and intensification of discrimination.
13 For more details on the issue, see The Voice Newspaper Online, 19 July 2023.
14 Phatsimo Kapeng, 2023. 'Government Vows to Church Pressure,' 14 August 2023.
15 Ibid.
16 UN Women: Global Database on Violence Against Women: Statistics from Botswana Police, 2003–2012.
17 My focus in this book is on what is by far the most common pattern of GBV: Violence perpetrated by men against women. As I will show, it is this pattern that is also most prominent in biblical accounts of GBV. This does not mean that other kinds of GBV—such as by men against men or boys, or by women against men, boys, girls, or women—are any less deserving of condemnation.
18 See Botswana Gender-based Violence Prevention and Support Center (BGBVC), 'Our History.'
19 Ibid.
20 Emang Basadi Association.
21 Grace's study also includes a focus on Nigeria where similar patterns are observed.
22 The Botswana Constitution with amendments through (2016).
23 Botswana (2022) International Religious Freedom Report, Executive Summary.
24 This is also the case elsewhere, e.g., in some other Protestant, Bible-emphasizing contexts, like in the US-led complementarianism movement (Cf. Grant Castleberry, 2015; Michelle Lee-Barnewall, 2016).

Bibliography

Amanze, J.N., 1994. *Handbook of Churches*. Gaborone: Pula Press.

Amanze, J.N., 2003. 'Christianity and Ancestor Veneration in Botswana.' *Studies in World Christianity* 9(1): 43–59.

Botlhoko, P., 2022. 'Johannesburg: Women's Underrepresentation in Politics in Botswana Remains the Lowest in SADC,' Mmegi Newspaper, 14 March 2022. Available at https://www.mmegi.bw/news/womens-underrepresentation-in-politics-causes-worry/news (Accessed 28 September 2023).

Botswana 2022 International Religious Report. Available at https://www.state.gov/wp-content/uploads/2023/05/441219-BOTSWANA-2022-INTERNATIONAL-RELIGIOUS-FREEDOM-REPORT.pdf (Accessed 28 September 2023).

Botswana Gender-based Violence Prevention and Support Center (BGBVC), 'Our History.' Available at https://www.bgbvc.org.bw/index.php/about/our-history (Accessed 29 September 2023).

Botswana Population Census, 2011. Available at https://www.statsbots.org.bw/sites/default/files/2011%20Population%20and%20housing%20Census.pdf (Accessed 19 September 2023).

Bott, S., Morrison, A. and Ellsberg, M., 2005. 'Preventing and Responding to Gender-based Violence in Middle and Low-income Countries: A Global Review and

Analysis.' Policy Research Working Paper; No. 3618. World Bank: Washington, DC. Available at http://hdl.handle.net/10986/8210 (Accessed 28 November 2023).

Cailleba, P. and Kumar, R.A., 2010. 'When Customary Laws Face Civil Society Organisations: Gender Issues in Botswana.' *African Journal of Political Science and International Relations* 9:330–339.

Campbell, E.K., 2006. Reflections on illegal immigration in Botswana and South Africa. *African Population Studies*, 21(2):1–23.

Castleberry, G. 2015. 'Complementarianism as a Movement.' Available at https://cbmw.org/2015/03/09/complementarianism-as-a-movement/ (Accessed 27 September 2023).

CIA World Fact Book, 2022.Botswana.Available at https://www.cia.gov/the-world-factbook/about/archives/2022/countries/botswana/#people-and-society (Accessed 10 June 2023).

Contributor, Pambazuka News, 'Botswaan: First Female Paramount Chief Welcomed,' 4 September 2003. Available at https://www.pambazuka.org/gender-minorities/botswana-first-female-paramount-chief-welcomed (Accessed 20 September 2023).

Denbow, J.R. and Thebe, P.C., 2006. *Culture and Customs of Botswana.* London: Greenwood Publishing Group.

Dube, M.W., 1999. 'Consuming a Colonial Cultural Bomb: Translating Badimo into "Demons" in the Setswana Bible (Matthew 8.28-34; 15.22; 10.8). *Journal for the Study of the New Testament* 21(73): 33–58. Available at https://doi.org/10.1177/0142064X9902107303 (Accessed 19 August 2023).

Dube, M.W., 2001. 'Divining Ruth for International Relations.' In Dube, M.W. (ed.) *Other Ways of Reading the Bible: African Women and the Bible.* Atlanta: SBL Press: 179–195.

Dube, M.W., 2003. 'Culture, Gender and HIV: Understanding and Acting on the Issues.' In Dube, M.W. (ed.) *HIV/AIDS and the Curriculum: Methods for Integrating HIV/AIDS in Theological Programs.* Geneva: World Council of Churches: 101–112.

Dube, M.W., 2012. 'Youth Masculinities and Violence in an HIV and AIDS Context: Sketches from Botswana Cultures and Pentecostal Churches.' In Chitando, E. and Chirongoma, S. (eds.) *Redemptive Masculinities: Men, HIV and Religion.* Geneva: World Council of Churches: 323–354.

Ellece, S.E., 2011. 'Be a Fool Like Me': Gender Construction in the Marriage Advice Ceremony in Botswana–A Critical Discourse Analysis.' *Agenda* 25(1): 43–52.

Ellece, S.E. and Rapoo, C., 2013. 'Who Should Teach Our Boys How to Respect Life? Theorising Volatile Gender Identities in Botswana.' *Marang: Journal of Language and Literature* 23: 59–73.

Emang Basadi Association, 2023. Available at https://awdf.org/emang-basadi-association-eba/ (Accessed 29 September 2023).

Exner, D. and Thurston, W.E., 2009. 'Understanding "Passion Killings" in Botswana: An Investigation of Media Framing.' *Journal of International Women's Studies* 10(4): 1–16.

Gabaitse, R.M., 2017. 'Luke 4: 18–19 and Salvation: Marginalization of Women in the Pentecostal Church in Botswana.' In Green, G.L., Pardue, S.T. and Yeo, K.K. (eds.) *So Great a Salvation: Soteriology in the Majority World.* Michigan: Eerdmans: 59–76.

Gobagoba, M.R. and Littrell, M.A., 2003. 'Profiling Micro Apparel Enterprises in Botswana: Motivations, Practices, Challenges, and Success.' *Clothing and Textiles Research Journal* 21(3): 130–141.

Good, K., 1993. 'At the Ends of the Ladder: Radical Inequalities in Botswana.' *The Journal of Modern African Studies* 31(2): 203–230.

Gouws, A. 2022. 'Violence against Women in South Africa Is Staggeringly High-a Different Way of Thinking about It Is Needed,' The Conversation, 29 November 2022. Available at https://theconversation.com/violence-against-women-is-staggeringly-high-in-southafrica-a-different-way-of-thinking-about-it-is-needed-195053#:~:text=South%20Africa%20has%20notoriously%20high,rape%20incidence%20in%20the%20world (Accessed 23 November 2023).

Grace, O.T., 2021. 'Addressing Gender-based Violence in Africa (Nigeria and Botswana).' *Saudi Journal of Humanities and Social Science* 6(10): 405–413.

Haron, M., 2007. 'The Demographics of Botswana's Christian Population and BC 200l.' In Nkomazana, F. and Lanner, L. (eds.) *Aspects of the History of the Church in Botswana*. Pietermaritzburg: Cluster Publications: 322–329.

Haron, M. and Jensen, K.E., 2008. 'Religion, Identity and Public Health in Botswana.' *African Identities* 6(2): 183–198.

Heise, L., Ellsberg, M. and Gottemoeller, M., 1999. *Ending Violence Against Women (Population Reports, Series L, No. 11)*. Baltimore: Johns Hopkins University School of Public Health, Center for Communications Programs.

Hitchcock, R.K., 2002. 'We Are the First People': Land, Natural Resources and Identity in the Central Kalahari, Botswana.' *Journal of Southern African Studies* 28(4): 797–824.

Kang'ethe, S.M., 2014. 'The Perfidy and Ramifications of Gender-based Violence (GBV) Meted against Women and the Girl Children in Botswana: A Literature Review.' *Mediterranean Journal of Social Sciences* 5(23): 1563–1567.

Kapeng, P., 2023. 'Government Vows to Church Pressure against LGBTIQ+ Rights,' 14 August 2023. Available at https://yourbotswana.com/2023/08/05/govt-bows-to-church-pressure-against-lgbtiq-rights/ (Accessed 30 September 2023).

Kebaneilwe, M.D., 2011. 'The Vashti Paradigm: Resistance as a Strategy for Combating HIV and AIDS.' *The Ecumenical Review* 63(4): 378–383.

Kebaneilwe, M.D. and Ellece, S.E., 2020. 'The Untold Story of Mrs Noah: The Hebrew Bible, Gender and Media: An Intertextual Critical Discourse Analysis.' *Boleswa Journal of Theology, Religion and Philosophy (BJTRP)* 5(2): 32–48.

Kgosikebatho, K. 2018. 'Murder, Rape on the Rise.' The Patriot on Sunday, September 28. Available at https://allafrica.com/stories/201809280260.html. (Accessed 1 April 2019).

Koss, M.P., 1993. 'Detecting the Scope of Rape: A Review of the Prevalence of Research Methods.' *Journal of Interpersonal Violence* 8(2): 198–222.

Kumar, R.A., 2010. 'Customary Law and Human Rights in Botswana: Accredited Survival of Conflicts.' *City University of Hong Kong Law Review* 2(2): 277–300.

Lebotse, T.D., 2009. *Victims or Actors of Development: The Case of the San People at D'kar, Botswana* (Master's thesis, Universitetet i Tromsø). Available at https://hdl.handle.net/10037/2402 (Accessed 18 October 2023).

Lee-Barnewall, M., 2016. *Neither Complementarian nor Egalitarian: A Kingdom Corrective to the Evangelical Gender Debate*. Michigan: Baker Academic.

Lekgowe, G.R., 2023, 'A New Dawn for Gay Rights in Botswana: A Commentary on the Decision of the High Court and Court of Appeal in the Motshidiemang Cases.' *Journal of African Law*: 1–9. Available at https://doi.org/10.1017/S0021855323000177 (Accessed 30 September 2023).

Lekobane, K.R. and Mooketsane, K.S., 2015. 'Examining Evidence of Feminization of Poverty in Botswana.' *Botswana Institute for Development Policy Analysis (BIDPA)*. Available at http://knowledge.bidpa.bw:8080/xmlui/handle/123456789/105 (Accessed 3 November 2022).

Lekoko, R.N. and Maruatona, T.L., 2006. 'Opportunities and Challenges of Widening Access to Education: Adult Education in Botswana.' In Oduaran, A. and Bhola, H.S. (eds.), *Widening Access to Education as Social Justice*. Dordrecht: Springer: 305–328. Available at https://doi.org/10.1007/1-4020-4324-4_19 (Accessed 19 August 2022).

Machisa, M. and van Dorp, R., 2012. *Gender Based Violence Indicators Study*. Gaborone: African Books collective.

Magang, D., 2015. *Delusions of Grandeur: Paradoxes and Ambivalences in Botswana's Macroeconomic Firmament* Gaborone: Print Media Consult.

Maundeni, T., 2002. 'Wife Abuse among a Sample of Divorced Women in Botswana: A Research Note.' *Violence Against Women* 8(2): 257–274.

Maundeni, T., 2016. 'Gender Equality and Women's Empowerment in Botswana: Progresses and Challenges.' In Awortwi, N. and Musahara, H. (eds.) *Implementation of the Millennium Development Goals: Progresses and Challenges in Some African Countries*. Addis Ababa: OSSREA: 139–162.

Mlilo, P., 2023. 'Protest Against Homosexuality: Churches Petition MP to Vote against Same-sex Relationships,' The Voice Newspaper Online, 19 July 2023. Available at https://thevoicebw.com/protest-against-homosexuality/ (Accessed 30 September 2023).

Moffat, R., 1842. *Missionary Labours in Southern Africa*. London: John Shaw.

Moffett, H., 2008. 'Sexual Violence, Civil Society and the New Constitution.' In Britton, H.E., Fish, J.N. and Meintj, S. (eds.) *Women's Activism in South Africa: Working Across Divides*. Durban: University of KwaZulu Natal Press: 155–184.

Mogalakwe, M., 2003. 'Botswana: An African Miracle or a Case of Mistaken Identity?' *Pula: Botswana Journal of African Studies* 17(1): 85–94.

Mogalakwe, M. and Nyamnjoh, F., 2017. 'Botswana at 50: Democratic Deficit, Elite Corruption and Poverty in the Midst of Plenty.' *Journal of Contemporary African Studies* 35(1): 1–14.

Mooketsane, K., Molefe, W., and Faiaz, M., et al., 2023. AD594: Batswana See Gender-based Violence as a Priority for Government and Societal Action. Afrobarometer. Available at https://www.afrobarometer.org/wp-content/uploads/2023/01/AD594-Botswana-see-gender-violence-as-a-priority-for-government-and-societal-action-Afrobarometer-18jan23.pdf (Accessed 28 September 2023).

Ncube, M., Lufumpa, C.L. and Vencatachellum, D., 2011. 'Gender in Employment: Case Study of Botswana.' *African Development Bank Group* 1(1): 1–28.

Newsom, C.A., 1989. 'Woman and the Discourse of Patriarchal Wisdom: A Study of Proverbs 1-9.' In Day, P.L. (ed.) *Gender and Difference in Ancient Israel*. Minneapolis: Fortress Press: 142–161.

Nkomazana, F., 2008. 'The Experiences of Women within Tswana Cultural History and Its Implications for the History of the Church in Botswana.' *Studia Historia Ecclesiasticae* 34(2): 83–119.

Ntseane, P., 2004. 'Being a Female Entrepreneur in Botswana: Cultures, Values, Strategies for Success.' *Gender and Development* 12(2): 37–43.

Online Editor, 'Mogae Wants War against 'Passion-Killings', Sunday Standard, 25 August 2013. Available at https://www.sundaystandard.info/mogae-wants-ocywaroco-against-ocypassion-killingsoco/ (Accessed 20 October 2023).

Owusu, F. and Samatar, A.I., 1997. 'Industrial Strategy and the African State: The Botswana Experience.' *Canadian Journal of African Studies/La Revue Canadienne des études Africaines* 31(2): 268–299.

Pambazuka News, 2004. "Botswana: First female Paramount Chief welcomed," 04 September, 2004. Available at https://www.pambazuka.org/gender-minorities/botswana-first-female-paramount-chief-welcomed (Accessed 28 September 2023).

Parliament of Botswana, 'About Ntlo ya Dikgosi.' Available at https://www.parliament.gov.bw/index.php/about-ntlo-ya-dikgosi (Accessed 20 September 2023).

Petrina, G.E., 2023. An Evaluation of Community Attitudes Towards Gender-Based Violence in Partnership with the Community of Maunatlala, Botswana. Oregon State University. Available at https://ir.library.oregonstate.edu/apa/8p58pn824 (Accessed 29 September 2023).

Quansah, E.K., 2005. 'Abolition of Marital Power in Botswana: A New Dimension in Marital Relationship?' *Botswana Law Journal* 1(1): 5–27.

Quansah, E.K., 2008. 'Law, Religion and Human Rights in Botswana: Focus: The Foundations and Future of Law, Religion and Human Rights in Africa.' *African Human Rights Law Journal* 8(2): 486–504.

Report on International Religious Freedom: Botswana (2022) Available at https://www.state.gov/reports/2022-report-on-international-religious-freedom/botswana (Accessed 10 0ctober 2022).

Robert, D.L., 2014. 'Gender Roles and Recruitment in Southern African Churches, 1996–2001.' In *Essamuah, C.B.* and *Ngaruiya, D.K.* (eds.) *Communities of Faith in Africa and the African Diaspora: In Honor of Dr. Tite Tienou with Additional Essays on World Christianity.* Oregon: Wifp and Stock Publishers: 116–128.

Schapera, I.S., 1966. *Married Life in an African Tribe.* Illinois: Northwestern University Press.

Selolwane, O.D., 2004. The Emang Basadi Women's Association. *Feminist Africa* (3): 1–5. Available at https://www.jstor.org/stable/48726030 (Accessed 29 September 2023)

Seng, M.P., 1992. 'In a Conflict Between Equal Rights for Women and Customary Law, the Botswana Court of Appeal Chooses Equality.' *University of Toledo Law Review* 24(3): 563–582.

Siphambe, H.K., 2000. 'Rates of Return to Education in Botswana.' *Economics of Education Review* 19(3): 291–300.

Statistics Botswana, 2022. 'Population and Housing Census 2022: Population of Cities, Towns and Villages.' Available at https://www.statsbots.org.bw/sites/default/files/2022%20Population%20and%20Housing%20Census%20Preliminary%20Results.pdf (Accessed 28 September 2023).

Sunday Standard Reporter, 'Only one Woman Elected to Ntlo ya Dikgosi,' 18 November 2019. Available at https://www.sundaystandard.info/only-one-woman-elected-to-ntlo-ya-dikgosi/ (Accessed 20 September 2023).

Swartz, N.P., Itumeleng, O.O. and Danga, A.M., et al., 2015. 'Is A Husband Criminally Liable for Raping His Wife? A Comparative Analysis.' *International Journal of Academic Research and Reflection* 3(3): 8–25.

Tabengwa, M. and Fergus, I.M., 1998. 'Violence against Women'. Paper Presented at the First National Crime Prevention Conference, Gaborone, Botswana. Available at https://www.africabib.org/rec.php?RID=W00096527 (Accessed 24 November 2023).

The Botswana Constitution with Amendments, 2016. Available at https://www.constituteproject.org/constitution/Botswana_2016 (Accessed 14 November 2022).

Tlou, T., 1985. *A History of Ngamiland: 1750 to 1906: The Formation of an African State*. Gaborone: Macmillan Botswana.

Togarasei, L., 2013. 'Christianity and Hegemonic Masculinities: Transforming Botswana Hegemonic Masculinity Using the Jesus of Luke.' *Scriptura: Journal for Contextual Hermeneutics in Southern Africa* 112(1): 1–12.

United Nations General Assembly Resolution 48/104, 1993. Declaration on the Elimination of Violence Against. Available at https://www.un.org/en/genocideprevention/documents/atrocity-crimes/Doc.21_declaration%20elimination%20vaw.pdf Accessed 6 September 2023.

United Nations, 1995. *Report of the Fourth World Conference on Women, Beijing 4-15 September 1995*. New York: United Nations.

United Nations' Refugee Agency, Gender-based Violence. 2020. Available at https://www.unhcr.org/what-we-do/protect-human-rights/protection/gender-based-violence (Accessed 09 September 2023).

United Nations Women, 1998. Global Database on Violence against Women-Botswana-Estimation of Rape Cases. Available at https://evaw-global-database.unwomen.org/fr/countries/africa/botswana/1998/cases-of-rape-and-violence-against-women (Accessed 19 October 2023).

Worldometer, 2023. 'Botswana Population.' Available at https://www.worldometers.info/world-population/botswana-population/ (Accessed 26 September 2023).

World Population Review, 2023. Rape Statistics by Country 2023. Available at https://worldpopulationreview.com/country-rankings/rape-statistics-by-country (Accessed 23 September 2023).

2 Establishing the Gaps
The Bible and GBV in Context

In the wake of surging media coverage, the subject of gender-based violence (GBV) has received increased scholarly attention. But given the sheer magnitude of GBV and its global reach, a lot more is urgently needed from *all* corners of the world, to muster and harness concerted effort and action to curb it. In a world so infested with horrific incidences, GBV remains one of the most prevalent manifestations of violence, to the detriment, particularly of women and girls (Morrison and Orlando 2004). Although efforts to address GBV in Africa continue, the powerful potential of faith actors (i.e., religious leaders, communities, resources, and organizations) is under-utilized. This book seeks to take a step towards redressing this. In this chapter, I seek to provide context: I will provide some overview of what has been done and achieved in my context of southern Africa, with a special focus on Botswana. Some reference will also be made to work elsewhere, which spotlights localized strategies towards combating GBV that take into consideration specific contexts. This will provide the foundation for the steps forward to be proposed later in this book.

GBV in the Bible: The Quest for Transformational Revelation

Many will agree that the Bible can be and has been used to justify acts of injustice. Indeed, some biblical texts describe or condone violence and injustices in multiple forms. As I will go on to argue, this is not the full story. I am not suggesting that the Bible is a "how to guide" or textbook for GBV. But problematic or violence-suggestive biblical texts need to be examined and, if necessary, exposed and shunned so that their influence, whether direct or otherwise, can be defused. If we do not confront such texts, harm, particularly to vulnerable members of our society, will go unchallenged. For instance, we know that rape becomes even more common in times of war. Men, too, are victims of wartime rape, but it is often women and girls who are targeted most (cf. Ashfold 2008; Hynes 2004; Lorentzen and Turpin 1998, 3). The Bible, too, describes rape in war (e.g., Lam. 5,11), and sometimes it makes allowances for and even permits rape as part of war (Num. 31:18; Deut. 21:10–14).

Now, if biblical war narratives condoning rape are not named and condemned, they could—explicitly or implicitly—contribute to downplaying the devastating impact of wartime rape. Wartime rape is not the focus of this book, but the power of texts is, and it should not be underestimated.

There is a move in biblical studies towards identifying and challenging the rape cultures reflected in and by biblical texts. Examples include the contributions in *Rape Culture, Gender Violence and Religion: Biblical Perspectives*.[1] The volume's editors, namely, Caroline Blyth, Emily Colgan and Katie Edwards maintain that "the Bible is a violent book whose contents bear witness to the pervasiveness of gendered violence in ancient Israel" (Blyth, Colgan and Edwards, 2018, 1). Another recent volume is *Rape Myths, the Bible, and #MeToo*,[2] which builds the case that inattention to rape in the Bible can perpetuate rape myths in contemporary cultures (Stiebert 2020,7). Similarly, Barbara Thiede's *Rape Culture in the House of David: A Company of Men* (Thiede 2022,1) maintains that sacred texts, including the Bible, underwrite contemporary rape cultures and that to romanticize, downplay or even ignore such has serious implications, particularly for communities of faith (Thiede 2022, 1). I concur that to turn a blind eye to GBV either in our life contexts, or in authoritative texts, like the Bible, will not only perpetuate but also permit GBV. As this book will show, GBV is rampant in both the Bible and in my community and must be named and eradicated. Moving closer to home, first to South Africa, and then to Botswana, let me mention the important work that has been and is continuing to be done to bring the Bible, its narratives, and images on GBV into conversation with southern African communities where GBV is also endemic.

The Ujamaa Centre: South Africa and Biblical Contextualization for Transformation

The Ujamaa Centre was established in 1989 at the University of KwaZulu-Natal in South Africa, with the aim to bridge the gap and create an interface between academic biblical studies (and theology) and biblical interpretations by local communities. The aim of this was to respond to and achieve a distinctive, contextually relevant form of liberation theology geared towards social justice and social transformation.[3] It must be understood that this was against the background of prevailing oppression and suffering of the people of South Africa during the apartheid regime. Prior to the Ujamaa Centre and also against the backdrop of the political crisis in South Africa, in 1985 there was the Kairos Document[4] which was a statement made primarily by Black South African theologians to challenge the church and all Christians in the country to act to disrupt and dismantle the system of apartheid in the quest to establish a just social system (Goba 1987, 134). The Ujamaa Centre was propelled by the similar ideals as those stated in the Kairos Document and aimed to snap the church and communities of faith out of their perceived inaction and silence in countering the socio-political ills suffered by Black South Africans in particular due to apartheid.

The Ujamaa Centre seeks to transform what they regard as sinful systems and structures that keep people oppressed. These include economic systems that ensure a wide gap between the poor and the rich, patriarchal systems that maintain male privilege, racialized systems that sustain white supremacy, and ecclesial systems that fail to confront injustices of all kinds.[5] The list of oppressions is long, and the aims of the Centre are commensurately diverse.

Famously, a method called Contextual Bible Study (CBS) was devised at the Ujamaa Centre. CBS facilitates the reading of biblical texts with participation and co-engagement between socially engaged scholars and ordinary readers (West 1991, 88). According to Gerald West (one of the pioneering members of the Ujamaa Centre as well as the CBS method), "ordinary readers" generally refers to non-scholars who have no academic training in biblical studies as opposed to tertiary trained scholars and theologians (West, 2007). These are usually the marginalized, poor, working-class grassroots communities of faith whose quest is to find a solution to their bread-and-butter issues from the Bible and its God.

Such Bible study deliberately applies selected biblical texts as the lens for discussing the circumstances and contexts of the participants present. Sometimes a CBS targets particular situations such as vulnerability to or living with GBV, HIV, or unemployment. One rationale for the method is that the Bible's relevance to participants' lives is self-evident. Benefits of the method include mobilization of grassroots activism, creating solidarity between different social groups, provision of training, individual and group empowerment, and support for marginalized communities, including through collaborating with communities of faith, government agencies, and civil society to promote social change for the good of all.

The manual, which was created collaboratively at the Ujamaa Centre,[6] is designed to train readers of the Bible to engage with the text in a variety of meaningful ways. These include the following: First, to appreciate the text's distinct voice rooted in its own socio-historical context; second, to help with reflection on the text's ongoing relevance for participants' own situations; and third, and most importantly, to use the same text as a tool in the quest for social transformation and against oppressive acts. The Centre is noted for one project which has particular relevance for me, given its focus on women, rape, and other manifestations of GBV. This is the Tamar Campaign, named after David's daughter, Tamar, who is raped by her brother Amnon (2 Samuel 13). The campaign was established specifically to help churches in breaking the silence and stigma around sexual violence and to address violent masculinities.[7] The campaign encourages readers and interpreters of the story of Tamar (and, by extension, of other such stories, for there are many accounts of rape in the Bible) to refrain from spiritualizing, rationalizing, or ignoring what happened to Tamar. To trivialize such a "text of terror"[8] is to silence victims, to collude with rapists, and, worse still, to promote repetition and recycling of the Bible's acceptance of rape in our own communities (Thiede 2022, 8).

The Tamar Campaign spread to other parts of Africa like Kenya, in East Africa, where it was established in 2005 by "The Fellowship of Christian Councils and Churches in the Great Lakes and the Horn of Africa" (FEC-CLAHA) (Nyabera et al. 2007). The Tamar Campaign sought to end GBV in Kenya and to address the missing voice of the church concerning the issue of rape.[9] It produced the *Contextual Bible Study Manual on Gender-based Violence*, edited by Fred Nyabera and Taryn Montgomery (2007). In this collection of essays, the editors offer an invitation to readers to consider GBV from a biblical perspective. The exercises in the book require exploration of biblical texts with instances of GVB, alongside exploration of the experiences of GBV by real flesh-and-blood human beings in contemporary communities of faith. By confronting GBV in biblical texts, readers are better able to identify with the texts on a deeper and more intimate level that allows them to see themselves and their GBV experiences from different and compassionate perspectives. As I shall demonstrate in the next chapter, the exercise opens new possibilities for healing and empowerment for victims and survivors of GBV in our contemporary contexts. This is encouraged as opposed to shying away from or defending GBV in biblical texts.

The CBS manual was designed for pastors, lay leaders, and different Bible groups, all of whom are encouraged to explore the positive and the negative potential and influence of specific biblical texts and to apply the messages of these texts towards healing in their own specific situations. This very much includes, alongside identifying harmful texts, a search for hope and for the love of God (Nyabera and Montgomery, 2007). Worth noting is that CBS has become over the past decades a trademark for African theologies and, emanating from there, across the world.[10] This is part of a changing trend that has moved towards greater inclusion, from privileging scholarly historical-critical readings of ancient sacred texts towards acknowledging also alternative readings, including those of diverse contemporary communities of faith.

For good reason, South Africa has been a very prominent focus for discussion on the interface between Bible and GBV. I say this because GBV is notoriously prevalent in South Africa,[11] and, alongside this, Christianity is the country's dominant religion, with the visibility of the Bible prevalent.[12] (I will later go on to make comparable claims for Botswana, which has been under-researched by comparison with South Africa.)

So, especially through the establishment of the Ujamaa Centre and the Tamar Campaign, a commendable amount of effort to address GBV using biblical texts has been and is continuing to be made in South Africa, and many hands are at work in this, making it impossible to name all of them here. Therefore, I will cursorily refer to the work of two more scholars from South Africa—and I admit that this is only a drop in the ocean. These two have, however, written extensively on issues related to the Bible and gender inequality and violence in their context. The examples used here are only illustrative and far from exhaustive.

I mention first Madipoane Masenya, who is a womanist South African biblical scholar, of Sotho descent. In her article "Without a Voice, with a Violated Body: Re-reading Judges to Challenge Gender-based Violence in Sacred Texts" (she explains that although women make up most of the population of South Africa, they are acutely vulnerable to violence (Masenya, 2012). According to Masenya, the violence is rooted in the country's multiple toxic patriarchies[13] which find expression in women's muted voices, in violent masculinities, and in violent biblical hermeneutics. When violent, oppressive, and gender-biased biblical texts are interpreted in predominantly patriarchal contexts, this results in further violence and oppression of women, she argues. In her reading of Judges 19, Masenya challenges GBV in both the biblical text as well as in her South African context (Masenya 2012, 205). Masenya is a prolific biblical scholar *and* someone who shows concern for her context and for making practical and positive change. Like the scholars working at the Ujamaa Centre, her scholarship is explicitly community-facing and activist.

The second South African biblical scholar I want to mention is another womanist scholar, this time of Indian descent, Sarojini Nadar. Nadar reads the book of Esther with special focus on the female characters Vashti and Esther. Again, she aims in her interpretation to advocate for social transformation and justice for women in South Africa. In her article "Gender, Power, Sexuality and Suffering Bodies in the Book of Esther" (Nadar 2002), Nadar confronts and dismantles oppressive gender and ethnic issues in the biblical text as they pertain to Vashti and Esther. She demonstrates, too, how the story can be read to empower and liberate women in her own context (Nadar 2002, 113). Given that many South African women (and this applies to many women across Africa) use the Bible as a "go-to" book in challenging times, it must be read, Nadar argues, for what is, without downplaying its violence, if it is to speak to the violated at all. Vashti and Esther are oppressed and sexually abused, and their voices are muted. As Nadar highlights, this is unacceptable—just as it is unacceptable in the case of contemporary women whose stories are mirrored in and by the biblical narrative. As Nadar further argues, when deconstructed, the story is capable of impacting "women living under the triple oppression of race, class, and gender in a very direct and pervasive manner" (Nadar 2002,113). Ultimately, a responsible and responsive reading is one that aims to unpack and expose whatever evil, and injustice is entrenched in sacred biblical texts, before repackaging the same with the aim to resist the evil and injustice and achieve liberation and healing in real-life South African contexts. Again, Nadar's work in this field is extensive, beginning with her PhD thesis (Nadar 2003) and right up to the present. Activism using the Bible, including for the purpose of achieving gender justice, has a long and strong heritage in South Africa.

Establishing the Gaps 37

Another recent volume entitled *The Bible and Gender Troubles in Africa* shows that while South Africa is in many ways a stronghold regarding activist Bible interpretation in the service of addressing gender inequalities and GBV, such interpretation is also gaining traction in other parts of the continent (Kuegler, Gabaitse and Stiebert 2019). While the volume contains many contributions by scholars from Zimbabwe, there is, however, no chapter focused on gender troubles in Botswana.

Let me digress briefly to mention the observation made by one of the volume's editors, Joachim Kügler, in his foreword, in reference to the conference that led to the production of the volume. The conference, also named "The Bible and gender troubles in Africa," was held in Zimbabwe in 2016, and Kügler makes the following observation about it:

… many of the male participants in Zimbabwe gave the impression that for them gender debates are something that should be fought against because they are something "unbiblical and un-African", threatening their masculinity. It is in this line that women (and men) standing up for gender justice often are attacked as "coconut" – brown on the outside, white on the inside. One sees them as agents of foreign Western agendas, which causes gender troubles … by inviting African women to challenge the traditional ideal of the submissive woman.

(Kügler, 2019: 8)

The above observation indicates that for some African men (and women), challenging gender inequality (as Masenya and Nadar do) is not only unbiblical but also un-African. This is important for my purpose in this book in that not only does it indicate that the battle for gender equality in Africa, generally, is still a dream yet to be realized but also, importantly, that there is, even more, a need to address the issue from a biblical perspective. The stance Kügler identifies here is what has propelled my current project to address particularly GBV from a perspective that seeks to *undress* the Bible and uncover the GBV entrenched in its narratives. My reason is that to bring it to the fore can allow for willingness to engage with GBV in my context, which is also infested with GBV. In other words, the Bible can legitimate the endeavor of examining GBV not only in the text but also in lived contexts. CBS at Ujamaa, Masenya and Nadar—all have made important links between texts held sacred and bodies that are also sacred, which need protection. All have legitimated and channeled activism to confront GBV.

The belief held by many Africans (men and women alike), as noted by Kügler above, that challenging gender inequality is both unbiblical and un-African points me to the need for uncovering gender injustice, both in our cultures (human cultures across the world and African, and Botswana culture) and in biblical texts. This can then open the possibility for a mutual conversation in both directions. That is, to counter the belief that gender inequality in both African (and other cultures) and biblical culture is normative, efforts must be made to expose not just the problem in contemporary cultures but in the biblical text as well. That is the gist of this book. My main argument is that GBV in the biblical texts should cease being a "no go" or grey area, to be avoided or spiritualized, including in church pulpits. Such a stance has aided and abetted the GBV crisis in my country.

Ezra Chitando, also in *The Bible and Gender Troubles in Africa*, maintains that from the missionary period to the present, the Church in Africa has interfaced with gender, for better or for worse (2019: 16). The Church, he argues, has endorsed patriarchy through a combination of conservative readings of the Bible and support for indigenous strands of patriarchy (Chitando, 2019,17). Sharing Chitando's sentiments, this book seeks to specifically explore GBV in Botswana, by retelling incidences of GBV in the Bible in the light of my *heavily* Christianized context of Botswana, in order not just to name the crimes but to seek heuristic ways to address them. This is based on my conviction that it is not possible to win a war against an enemy unless one knows exactly who that enemy is and how they operate. Consequently, I endeavor to explore the possible collusion between the Bible (as an authoritative, highly respected book of life in Botswana) and Botswana culture about GBV by naming specific incidences and critically engaging with them.

However, this is not to undermine the efforts of Batswana scholars, activists, and others working within Botswana, who have also contributed to addressing gender inequality with the Bible. Such practice is not as extensive as in South Africa, even if the urgency is as great. In the next section, therefore, I want to turn my focus to a sample of what some scholars working within Botswana have achieved. This is to show that my current work, in this book, is building on an existing foundation, but this time with a special focus on how the Bible interfaces with GBV in my context. Notable too is that many factors come into play when dealing with issues of gender inequality in southern Africa, such as colonial and indigenous forms of racism, sexism, and the legacies of apartheid. What follows will demonstrate that factors such as HIV and AIDS, colonial imperialistic history, and its aftermath also play into the discussion in the Botswana context, but my focus will turn increasingly to GBV against women.

What Has Preceded: Efforts to Confront the Patriarchal Status Quo in Both the Bible and Setswana Culture

In Botswana, as in much of sub-Saharan Africa, the Bible is held in high esteem, and this has been noted already in the previous chapter. What must be understood clearly is that for a long time, and up into the present, the Bible has been interpreted, especially by spiritual leaders, selectively and with a tendency to literalism. This has served to maintain a patriarchal status quo evidenced in both Christian and African traditions that promotes male dominance over women. However, for more than three decades now, this trend has been challenged and confronted, including by scholars of the Bible from Botswana. The work of renowned Motswana New Testament biblical scholar Musa Dube has been pivotal. While trained beyond her first degree in academic institutions in the West (the UK and USA), Dube remains firmly rooted in the Botswana context, and her research is informed by her personal and complex experiences of being a woman in Botswana. Dube began her long journey of re-reading biblical texts from a feminist post-colonial perspective that aims to decolonize the Bible as well as to depatriarchalize its content. She "crafts a liberation approach to scripture that encounters the canon both as an imperialistic text, and a text for liberation" (Browning 2011, 5). While Dube's extensive work is impossible to summarize here, I want to turn attention to her important work of reading the Bible alongside Batswana women's experiences.

Navigating the overwhelmingly androcentric biblical narratives, Dube manages to call attention to female characters in the texts. She does so with a view to real women with real issues, in this case, Batswana women, by encouraging them to see themselves and put their experiences into perspective alongside biblical women characters. In so doing, biblical characters are made to speak to real flesh-and-blood women, with real-life predicaments, pertaining to their muted voices, marginalized existence, oppression, and victimization. During the peak of the HIV and AIDS pandemic, when its ravaging effects were at their worst, with sub-Saharan Africa being hardest hit (cf. UNAIDS 2000), Dube developed a new reading strategy in her quest to find life-affirming messages in the Bible while forces of death intensified all around. Her article "Talita Cum: Calling the Girl-Child and Women to Life in the HIV and Globalization Era" tackles the question of how the Bible can empower women and girl-children to persist and insist on life against the entwined forces of both globalization and HIV/AIDS that otherwise curtail their choices and prospects (2003:11). For this, she uses the story of the bleeding woman and the dying girl in Mark 5:23–43. In both stories, readers are confronted with desperate patients who have been sick for a long time without any help and with parents who have watched their children's suffering and death (Dube 2003, 19). As Dube asserts, the stories highlight gender disparities in that while men are named (Jairus, Peter, and John) women are nameless. The bleeding woman is identified only by her condition, which in this case signals her marginal status as unclean; the identity of the daughter of Jairus is tied to her father, while her mother, at home watching and caring for her, is not recognized by the text at all. The story further exposes power abuse typical in a globalized world where the rich exploit the poor in that the supposed physicians who attended to the bleeding woman only worsened her status by taking her money in charging her for what they could get, like what AIDS patients experienced before the antiretrovirals (ARVs) were discovered. Significantly, Dube closes her reading with life-changing questions, asking the audience and readers to find themselves in the story (Dube 2003).

Since globalization is driven by the quest for the global market and maximization of profits, it creates cultural and economic insecurity and threatens male power both politically and economically. When that happens, the tendency for men is to double down on their dominance over and oppression of women (Dube 2003, 12). The effects of globalization, coupled with those of HIV and AIDS, compromised the chances of empowerment for women and girls who, as statistics show, are also the most vulnerable and most affected by the latter (ibid; UNAIDS and UNDP 2001).

Important for my purpose in this book is that globalization and HIV/AIDS in intensifying women's oppression have also led to more GBV against women.[14] The massive toll of the pandemic in its early years before the availability of ARV treatments saw many women getting infected and succumbing to the disease, not least, because their right to negotiate safe sex was disregarded.[15] The strains imposed by HIV/AIDS led to more GBV (as would, later, the strains imposed by the COVID-19 pandemic). These were facilitated at least in part by *misguided* patriarchal ideology that men own, or are entitled to, women's bodies—with the Bible widely applied to justify such ideology. The point will be explored further in Chapter 3. Let me hasten to explain that with the wide availability of ARVs, AIDS is now kept at bay, and HIV is under control, with the virus no longer decimating life expectancy, as it did early in the millennium. GBV, however, is flaring up and needs urgent attention—hence this is where my focus lies.

Dube's emphasis on real women in her biblical research and her purposeful aim to procure positive change in Botswana society are vital and inspiring to my own line of research, as I aim to tackle the GBV crisis. I want to underline that Dube's scholarship has been pivotal in Botswana, pioneering a contextual biblical hermeneutics that gives attention to Batswana faith communities' situational contexts in their reading of texts. As she makes so abundantly clear, reading and interpretation of biblical texts must be purposeful and intentional, targeting positive transformation of the socio-political, economic, and cultural landscape of the receivers of the texts. Efforts must be aimed towards life-affirming readings of biblical texts that begin with seeing and acknowledging the religio-cultural, economic, and socio-political ills present in the texts as a reflection of the same in the real world. That is the first step towards the life-affirming biblical hermeneutics that this book advocates for. Taking the lead from Dube, I will direct her methods and advocacy toward an urgent problem in Botswana's present: GBV.

Another New Testament scholar from Botswana, Rosinah Gabaitse, also takes strides forward in the effort to empower biblical readers in Botswana. Her strategies read for women's empowerment by tackling the toxic masculinities apparent in both biblical texts and Botswana culture. In her chapter on "Passion Killings in Botswana: Masculinity at Crossroads" (2012), Gabaitse explains that churches in Botswana are patriarchal and promote and teach male superiority and female subordination. Church leaders have embraced the androcentrism prevalent in biblical texts without giving much thought to how damaging that is to relationships between men and women. Gabaitse maintains that it is time churches become intentional about teaching and promoting life-giving masculinities and refraining from favoring those biblical texts that promote gender inequality. Instead, she argues, church teaching should shift attention to texts that teach equality—for the good of both men and women (2008: 320). Furthermore, the church might help towards facilitating life-affirming masculinities by promoting such in their Sunday school curricula so that children learn from an early age about gender justice. Gabaitse also recommends that pastors seize the opportunity of standing at the church pulpit every Sunday to use this platform to "denounce violence against women" (Gabaitse 2012, 321). In this essay, Gabaitse makes an important if very general appeal to churches to step up to challenge gender inequality, which she convincingly blames on violent masculinities within Setswana culture. She observes that churches tend to emphasize and promote the patriarchal culture of biblical texts and selectively teach on those parts and interpretations of biblical scripture that advocate for male supremacy and female subordination. Gabaitse, like me, recognizes selective African and Christian traditions as endorsing hegemonic masculinities. But we both also see other traditions that can be raised up instead to resist these.

Gabaitse's call for a deconstruction of violent masculinities is just the beginning of more much-needed efforts to address gender inequality and GBV using the very Bible that is overtly and overwhelmingly male biased in its subject matter and applications. The trick for me is to find creative, persuasive, and convincing ways of reading biblical texts that show first, how biblical texts are riddled with gender inequality and other forms of violence; second, why these must be named, deconstructed, and carefully analyzed; and third, how to transform them into life-affirming messages that might indeed lie hidden amid the terror of violence, injustice, discrimination, and marginalization.

Sidney Berman, a scholar of the Old Testament from Botswana who is also a church leader, in his article "Of God's Image, Violence Against Women and Feminist Reflections" (Berman 2015) reads the biblical Book of Hosea and reflects on how it resonates with GBV in Botswana. Berman's reading finds a connection between Christian teachings as exemplified in Hosea and Setswana tradition-cultural orientations and socialization. Together the two traditions provide fertile soil for GBV to the detriment of women and girls. Not only does Hosea present a dichotomous view of men and women in which men are superior while women are inferior but it also presents a skewed view of women and their sexuality as devious (Berman 2015).[16]

The threats of violence against Gomer, the woman in Hosea, by her intimate partner/husband resonate with the Botswana context in which rates of intimate partner violence and femicide are high. According to Berman, the text allows the man-prophet Hosea to beat Gomer, to strip her naked in public, to humiliate her[17] and worse still, this is used as a metaphor for God in his dealings with his people Israel whom Gomer symbolizes (Berman 2015). The Book of Hosea sadly presents readers with a violent God who is an abuser of his wife (Israel) and even worse, God tolerates no divorce.[18] Berman concludes that there is a disturbing agreement between the biblical text and GBV in Setswana traditional culture. What intrigues me is that Berman exposes the injustice done to the female character by the male perpetrator allowing readers to see that a biblical text is full of inhumane acts that must be named before they can be addressed in real-time. His reading from a feminist perspective is also impressive, as it encourages other Batswana men (and men everywhere), those, like himself, in church leadership, to understand that the Bible needs to be read with caution and be critiqued in search of life-affirming messages instead of being taken literally when it is so damaging to do so. In a nutshell, "because the Bible says so" does not make it right. Berman is advocating for what I am pursuing in this book: Making the biblical text relevant to the Botswana context, with a particular focus on GBV.

Some of my earlier work has also prepared me for the topic. Reading the book of Esther with the aim to empower Batswana women in my article "The Vashti Paradigm: Resistance as a Strategy for Combating HIV and AIDS", I call attention to Vashti's legacy of resistance to male power and oppression (Kebaneilwe 2011). In part because of the patriarchal nature of Botswana culture, many Batswana women, particularly in the earlier years of the pandemic, succumbed to AIDS. Batswana men, much like their biblical counterparts in the narrative of Esther, hold the idea that they own women's bodies, denying women the freedom to negotiate safe sex. Therefore, from the story of Vashti, Batswana women, like others who live under tyrannical rule, can find strength and affirmation (Kebaneilwe 2011, 381–382). As I explore there, "The resistance model offered by Vashti is especially relevant to those women in marriages in Africa where the husband does what he pleases, including being promiscuous and risking infecting his wife with the virus." The paper specifically addresses the issue of women's oppression both in the biblical narrative of the book of Esther and in the Botswana context of HIV and AIDS. Here I will revisit some of these earlier ideas and direct them toward tackling the current GBV pandemic.

In another article titled "The Untold Story of 'Mrs Noah': The Hebrew Bible, Gender and Media: An Intertextual Critical Discourse Analysis" (2020), my colleague Sibonile Ellece and I maintain that in the notoriously androcentric narratives of the Bible, women's stories are either abbreviated or erased (Kebaneilwe and Ellece 2020). Reading the mythical story of Noah in Genesis 6–9, we note that his wife is not only unnamed but she is also voiceless and only exists as a foil in the shadow of her famous husband. We see resonance between this and our own context of Botswana where women's stories of suffering and courage hardly receive an audience. Instead, in both contexts, women are instead often negatively represented, as adulteresses, wicked tricksters, and temptresses.[19] Through an intertextual womanist lens, we critically analyze the discourse of Noah's story in which Mrs Noah is but a footnote, alongside the poem of the "Woman of Courage"[20] of Proverbs 31:10–31 and Batswana women's forgotten stories. We argue that Mrs Noah like the woman of Proverbs 31 "must have served, helped, and ministered to all her household, her husband and children." Given that her husband was an absent father who spent all his time doing God's work, leaving all family matters in the hands of his wife, she too deserves credit for her nurture and hard work.[21] Mrs Noah's unrecognized presence and deeds remind us of the story of three Batswana chiefs, all men: Khama III, Bathoen I, and Sebele I, remembered and honored for their efforts that led to Botswana's independence from British rule in 1966 (cf. Makgala 2008,89). While the three are well known, written about in Botswana's history books, with statues erected to their memory, and their images on Botswana's 100 Pula bank note, their wives, mothers, and any other women in their lives are hardly mentioned. Tellingly, the stories of the women who nurtured and supported them mean next to nothing to the curators of history; they are simply buried and forgotten. Like their biblical fellow matriarch, Mrs Noah, the wives of the three Batswana chiefs are not credited for the domestic jobs they performed for their husbands and families. Again, I will be building on this earlier work of making visible what is too often left invisible or obscured. I will argue that biblical texts are neither blameless in the surge of GBV nor powerless to act as tools of resistance.

No Recycling of Biblical Injustices: Read It, Name It, and Fix It

Reading biblical texts with a mind to gather anything and everything useful and of value towards mending a broken world must begin with naming. Naming in this case refers to overtly acknowledging, pointing out, and calling out the ills present in biblical texts. We must expose violence, including GBV, sexual violence, violence against minorities, violence against the environment, marginalization of vulnerable groups, the list goes on!—and only then can we confront and defeat it. Identifying violence in biblical texts, moreover, can act as a mirror for acknowledging our own violent environment. The Bible as mirror can help us better see what must change. And my focus here is on change to resist GBV.

As cursorily summarized in this chapter, I am building on an existing foundation. In South Africa and in my own country, Botswana, there are religious leaders and scholars, lawmakers, and activists working to address social problems. I want to add my voice and take this forward by centering the Bible on GBV. Why? First, because the Bible contains accounts of GBV, which legitimates naming, discussing, and confronting such violence. Second, because the biblical characters we read about, feel for, cry with, or applaud can compel us to reflect on real flesh-and-blood human players and actors in our contemporary societies. This is so because in Botswana, the Bible holds authority and commands attention. Readers of the Bible seek meaning and guidance from the Bible and sometimes attach emotions to characters in biblical narratives—even though, if they ever lived, they lived so very long ago.

And so, I wish to use the Bible to address GBV in Botswana. In this, I am drawing on and giving tribute to the work of predecessors, notably, collaborators at the Ujamaa Centre, and socially engaged biblical scholars of southern Africa, including Botswana. When Dube reads the stories of the bleeding woman and of Jairus' daughter in the gospel of Mark, she first acknowledges them as reflections of what transpires in her own context. Making the text present in her setting and naming shared pain lead her reading onwards to a deeper level where the audience is required to reflect on their own actions, the actions of others, and to name themselves in the text they are reading. In that way, the biblical text can speak to real people and situations, which can lead to much-needed transformation. In pursuit of social transformation in the face of GBV in Botswana, I will next explore a selection of biblical texts: Genesis 1–3, Judges 19–21, 2 Samuel 13, and the Book of Esther. These texts will be examined alongside cases of GBV in Botswana as reported in five national newspapers.

Notes

1 Edited by Caroline Blyth, Emily Colgan, and Katie B. Edwards. Palgrave Macmillan, 2018.
2 By Johanna Stiebert. London: Routledge, 2020.
3 For information about the Ujamaa Centre and for open-access resources, including the Contextual Bible Study manual, see their website.
4 For more information on the Kairos Document (1985), https://kairossouthernafrica.wordpress.com/2011/05/08/the-south-africa-kairos-document-1985/
5 See http://ujamaa.ukzn.ac.za.
6 Available on the Ujamaa Centre website, http://ujamaa.ukzn.ac.za.
7 Ibid.
8 The designation "texts of terror" was famously used by Phyllis Trible in her seminal book titled *Texts of Terror: Literary-Feminist Readings of Biblical Narratives* (1984). In the book, Trible critically engages with the sad stories of terror and violence against women in four biblical narratives namely, the gang rape and dismemberment of the Levite's concubine (Judges 19); the rape of Tamar by her half-brother Amnon (2 Samuel 13); the sacrifice of Jephthah's daughter to fulfil a vow made to God (Judges 11:29–40), and the use, sexual abuse, and expulsion of Hagar (Genesis 16–21).
9 Lott Carey, 'The Tamar Campaign to End Gender-based Violence Initiative.'
10 For example, in his seminal article titled 'African Biblical Studies: An Introduction to an Emerging Discipline' (2017), Andrew Mbuvi explains at length the contextual nature of biblical studies in Africa as a whole. Noteworthy too is that while CBS is commonly associated with African scholars reading biblical texts to make them speak to their intimate, real contexts of poverty, disease, gender inequality etc., the same is being done throughout the world as exemplified in Johanna Stiebert's recent publication on *Rape Myths, the Bible and #METOO* (2019) in which she engages critically with biblical texts to expose the rampancy of rape culture in the texts and in her Western context with the aim to confront such violence as

exposed in the #METOO movement. The list of such is endless and hopefully deferrable from the content of this chapter.
11 See Saferspaces 2023. 'Gender-based Violence in South Africa.'
12 For a more comprehensive summary of the prevalence of the Bible in South Africa, see Gerald West, *The Stolen Bible: From Tool of Imperialism to African Idol* (2016). West has published widely on this topic, but this is his magnum opus.
13 Reference to patriarchies and not just patriarchy (in the singular) is used here by Masenya to denote the diverse ethnic and racial groups in South Africa, each with their own patriarchal identities. That is, South Africa is comprised of Black Africans who make up much of its demography, followed by Coloured, White, and Indian communities. For further information on this, see Natalie Cowling 2023. 'Total Population of South Africa by Ethnic Groups.'
14 According to the Fifth Botswana AIDS Impact Survey (BAIS V) of September 2022, HIV prevalence was 26.2% among females and 15.2% among males. This corresponds with Jonathan Gichaara 2008. 'Women, Religio-cultural Factors and HIV/AIDS in Africa,' p. 194, who notes that of the 29.4 million people living with AIDS in sub-Saharan Africa, women constitute 58% of those between the ages of 15 and 49.
15 Mmapula D. Kebaneilwe 2011. 'The Vashti Paradigm.' In this article, I have demonstrated that in Botswana, women have no acceptable right to negotiate sex issues with their intimate male partners. This is evidenced by the country's law, which does not recognize marital rape. As a result of such damaging cultural practices, women, especially married ones, have succumbed to the menace of HIV and AIDS where their unfaithful partners or spouses infected them. See also, Jonathan Gichaara 2008. 'Women, Religio-cultural Factors.' He argues that the scourge of HIV/AIDS pandemic is particularly thriving among women because of the patriarchal African culture. He further explains that the virus is driven by male predatory sexual behaviour while the culture, particularly in sub-Saharan Africa (where Botswana is located), does not allow women to say "no" to male sexual overtures; women are expected culturally to oblige to their men's sexual demands without question.
16 Worth noting is that Hosea has long been the focus of feminist and womanist writers, including Renita J. Weems 1995. *Battered Love*; Gale A. Yee 1992. 'Hosea.'
17 This case of publicly stripping women naked has a dreadful legacy even in Botswana (cf. Mmapula D. Kebaneilwe 2021. 'Jesus as a Victim of Sexual Violence.'
18 For more details on the idea that God does not tolerate divorce, see Phillippe Denis 2002. 'Breaking the Covenant of Violence Against Women.'
19 In Botswana society (as in some other parts of the world), the media perpetuates and supports gender-oppressive discourses. For instance, in 2007, a Motswana woman politician who was aspiring to become the leader of a political party was portrayed in the media, in a national newspaper, as a castrated and bleeding animal. She was made a laughingstock because she was competing for a position culturally reserved for men. Being a woman is equated to being weak and incapable of leadership. For details on this, see Akpabio 2008. 'The Kathleen Letshabo Cartoon Controversy: An Online Audit.'
20 The title 'woman of courage' is my own translation of the Hebrew *eshet hayil*, the phrase used to describe the woman of Proverbs 31:10–31. For further details, see Mmapula D. Kebaneilwe 2012. 'This Courageous woman.'
21 Bringing out of the shadows and celebrating invisibilized women is an important practice in African womanist interpretation (Cf. Makhosazana Nzimande, 'Reconfiguring Jezebel'). Nzimande draws attention not only to Jezebel but also to Naboth's wife who is completely written out of the story.

Bibliography

Akpabio, E., 2008. 'The Kathleen Letshabo Cartoon Controversy: An Online Audit.' *Gender and Media Diversity Journal* 5: 45–50.

Ashford, M.W., 2008. 'The Impact of War on Women.' In Levy, B.S. and Sidel, V.W. (eds.) *War and Public Health*. Oxford: Oxford University Press: 186–196.

Berman, S.K., 2015. 'Of God's Image, Violence against Women and Feminist Reflections.' *Studia Historiae Ecclesiasticae* 41(1): 122–137.

Blyth, C., Colgan, E. and Edwards, K.B. (eds.), 2018. *Rape Culture, Gender Violence, and Religion: Biblical Perspectives*. London: Palgrave Macmillan.

Browning, M., 2011. 'Hanging Out a Red Ribbon: Listening to Musa Dube's Postcolonial Feminist Theology.' *Journal of Race, Ethnicity, and Religion* 2(13): 1–27.

Chirawu, S., 'Till Death Do Us Part: Marriage, HIV/AIDS and the Law in Zimbabwe.' *Cardozo JL and Gender* 13: 23. Available at http://law.bepress.com/expresso/eps/1419. (Accessed 25 March 2023).

Chitando, E., 2019. 'Introduction: The Bible, the Church and Gender Troubles in Africa.' In Kügler, J., Gabaitse, R. and Stiebert, J. (eds.) *The Bible and Gender Troubles in Africa*. Bamberg: University of Bamberg Press: 13–24.

Cowling, N., 2023. 'Total Population of South Africa by Ethnic Groups.' Available at https://www.statista.com/statistics/1116076/total-population-of-south-africa-by-population-group/ (Accessed 23 August 2023).

Denis, P., 2002. 'Breaking the Covenant of Violence against Women.' *Journal of Theology for Southern Africa* 114: 5–17.

Dlamini, N.Z.P., 2022. 'Unmasking Christian Women Survivor Voices against Gender-based Violence: A Pursuit for a Feminist Liberative Pastoral Care Praxis for Married Women in the Anglican Church of Southern Africa.' PhD diss. University of KwaZulu Natal, Pietermaritzburg. Available at https://researchspace.ukzn.ac.za/server/api/core/bitstreams/cc049958-55c2-44d0-9d82-cc47e067fb39/content (Accessed 27 March 2023).

Dube, M.W., 2010. 'Go Tla Siama. O Tla Fola: Doing Biblical Studies in an HIV and AIDS Context.' *Black Theology* 8(2): 212–241.

Dube, M.W., 2003. Talitha cum! Calling the girl-child and women to life in the HIV/Aids and globalization era. In Masenya, M., Phiri, I. A. and Haddad, B. *African Women, HIV/AIDS and Faith Communities*, Pietermaritzburg: Cluster Publications: 71–93.

Gabaitse, R.M., 2015. 'Pentecostal Hermeneutics and the Marginalisation of Women.' *Scriptura: Journal for Contextual Hermeneutics in Southern Africa* 114(1): 1–12.

Gabaitse, R.M., 2017. 'Luke 4: 18–19 and Salvation: Marginalization of Women in the Pentecostal Church in Botswana.' In Green, G.L., Perdue, S.T. and Yeo, K. (eds.) *So Great a Salvation: Soteriology in the Majority World*. Carlisle: Langham: 59–76.

Gabaitse, R.M., 2012. Passion killings in Botswana: Masculinity at crossroads. *Redemptive Masculinities: Men, HIV and Religion*. Geneva: WCC Publications: 305–321.

Gichaara, J., 2008. 'Women, Religio-cultural Factors and HIV/AIDS in Africa.' *Black Theology* 6(2): 188–199.

Goba, B., 1987. 'The Kairos Document and Its Implications for Liberation in South Africa.' *Journal of Law and Religion* 5(2): 313–325.

Hynes, H.P., 2004. 'On the Battlefield of Women's Bodies: An Overview of the Harm of War to Women.' *Women's Studies International Forum* 27(5–6): 431–445.

Kebaneilwe, M.D., 2011. 'The Vashti Paradigm Resistance as a Strategy for Combating HIV.' *The Ecumenical Review* 63(4): 378–383.

Kebaneilwe, M.D., 2012. 'This Courageous woman: A Socio-rhetorical Womanist Reading of Proverbs 31: 10–31.' PhD diss., Murdoch University. Available at http://researchrepository.murdoch.edu.au/id/eprint/16159 (Accessed 30 September 2023).

Kebaneilwe, M.D., 2018. 'Reading the Book of Esther in the Light of Botswana's 21st-Century Challenges.' *BOLESWA Journal of Theology, Religion and Philosophy (BJTRP)* 5(1): 52–64.

Kebaneilwe, M.D., 2021. 'Jesus as a Victim of Sexual Abuse: A Womanist Critical Discourse Analysis of the Crucifixion.' In Reaves, J.R., Tombs, D. and Figueroa, R. (eds.) *When Did We See You Naked? Acknowledging Jesus as a Victim of Sexual Abuse*. London: SCM Press: 230–248.

Kebaneilwe, M.D. and Ellece, S., 2020. 'The Untold Story of "Mrs Noah": The Hebrew Bible, Gender, and Media: An Intertextual Critical Discourse Analysis.' *Boleswa Journal of Theology, Religion and Philosophy (BJTRP)* 5(2): 32–48.

Krug, E.G., Mercy, J.A., Dahlberg, L.L. and Zwi, A.B., 2002. 'The World Report on Violence and Health.' *The Lancet* 360(9339): 1083–1088.

Kügler, J., 2019. 'Foreword.' In Kuegler, J., Gabaitse R. and Stiebert J. (eds.) *The Bible and Gender Troubles in Africa*. Vol. 22. Bamberg: University of Bamberg Press: 7–11.

Kügler, J., Gabaitse, R. and Stiebert, J. eds., 2019. *The Bible and Gender Troubles in Africa* (Vol. 22). Bamberg: University of Bamberg Press.

Lorentzen, L.A. and Turpin, J.E. (eds.), 1998. *The Women and War Reader*. New York: NYU Press.

Lott Carey, 'The Tamar Campaign to End Gender-based Violence Initiative.' Available at https://lottcarey.org/the-tamar-campaign/ (Accessed 20 May 2023).

Makgala, C.J., 2008. 'The Historical and Politico-cultural Significance of Botswana's Pula Currency.' *Pula: Botswana Journal of African Studies* 22(1): 41–55.

Masenya, M., 2012. 'Without a Voice, with a Violated Body: Re-reading Judges 19 to Challenge Gender Violence in Sacred Texts.' *Missionalia: Southern African Journal of Mission Studies* 40(3): 205–216.

Mbubi, A., 2017. 'African Biblical Studies: An Introduction to an Emerging Discipline' in.' *Currents in Biblical Research* 15(2): 149–178.

Morrison, A. and Orlando, M.B., 2004. 'The Costs and Impacts of Gender-based Violence in Developing Countries: Methodological Considerations and New Evidence.' Available at http://gender.careinternationalwikis.org/_media/morrisonorlandogenderbasedviolence.pdf

Nadar, S., 2002. 'Gender, Power, Sexuality and Suffering Bodies in the Book of Esther: Reading the Characters of Esther and Vashti for the Purpose of Social Transformation.' *Old Testament Essays* 15(1): 113–130.

Nadar, S., 2003. *Power, Ideology and Interpretation/s: Womanist and Literary Perspectives on the book of Esther as Resources for Gender-social Transformation* (Doctoral dissertation). Available at http://hdl.handle.net/10413/3449 (Accessed 23 July 2023).

Nyabera, F. and Montgomery, T., 2007. *Contextual Bible Study Manual on Gender-based Violence*. Nairobi: The Fellowship of Christian Councils and Churches in the Great Lakes and The Horn of Africa. (FECCLAHA).

Nzimande, M.K., 2008. 'Reconfiguring Jezebel: A Postcolonial Imbokodo1 Reading of The Story of Naboth's Vineyard (I Kings 21: 1–16).' In de Wit, H. and West, G.O. (eds.) *African and European Readers of the Bible in Dialogue*. Leiden: Brill: 223–258.

Omenyo, C.N., 2014. 'African Pentecostalism.' In Cecil, M. and Young, A.M. (eds.) *The Cambridge Companion to Pentecostalism*. Cambridge: Cambridge University Press: 132–151.

Pype, K., 2015. 'The Liveliness of Pentecostal/Charismatic Popular Culture in Africa.' In Martin, K.L. (ed.) *Pentecostalism in Africa*. Leiden: Brill: 345–378.

Reed, E., Raj, A., Miller, E. and Silverman, J.G., 2010. 'Losing the "Gender" in Gender-based Violence: The Missteps of Research on Dating and Intimate Partner Violence.' *Violence Against Women* 16(3): 348–354.

Saferspaces, 2023. 'Gender-based Violence in South Africa.' Available at https://www.saferspaces.org.za/understand/entry/gender-based-violence-in-south-africa (Accessed 23 September 2023).

Stiebert, J., 2020. *Rape Myths, the Bible, and# MeToo*. London: Routledge/Taylor & Francis.

The Kairos Document: A Challenge to Action, 1985. Available at https://kerkargief.co.za/doks/bely/GD_Kairos.pdf (Accessed 12 June 2023).

Thiede, B., 2022. *Rape Culture in the House of David: A Company of Men*. London: Routledge, Taylor & Francis.

Ujamaa Centre for Biblical and Theological Community Development and Research. Available at http://ujamaa.ukzn.ac.za (Accessed 14 April 2023).

UNAIDS and UNDP, 2001. 'Summary of the Declaration of Commitment on HIV/AIDS.' Available at https://www.unaids.org/sites/default/files/sub_landing/files/jc668-keepingpromise_en.pdf (Accessed 12 June 2023).

UNAIDS, 2000. 'Report on the Global AIDS Epidemic.' Available at https://www.unaids.org/en/resources/documents/2000/20000619_2000_gr. (Accessed 12 June 2023).

Weems, R.J., 1995. *Battered Love: Marriage, Sex, and Violence in the Hebrew Prophets*. Minneapolis: Fortress Press.

West, G.O., 1991. 'The Relationship between Different Modes of Reading (the Bible) and the Ordinary Reader.' *Scriptura: Journal for Biblical, Theological and Contextual Hermeneutics* 9: 87–110.

West, G.O., (ed.), 2007. *Reading Otherwise: Socially Engaged Biblical Scholars Reading With Their Local Communities*. No. 62. Atlanta: Society of Biblical Literature.

Yee, G.A., 1992. 'Hosea.' In Newsom, C.A. and Ringe, S.H. (eds.) *The Women's Bible Commentary*. London: SCPK: 195–202.

3 Gender-based Violence
Endemic in Biblical Texts and in Botswana Context

Chapter 1 set the scene, and illustrated some of the ways biblical and traditional Setswana gender ideologies conspire, to the detriment of Batswana women and girls. Chapter 2, meanwhile, summarized ways in which the Bible has already been read and instrumentalized with liberatory purpose in both Botswana and neighboring South Africa. Contextual Bible Study (CBS), as discussed, is one well-established, distinctively southern African method of socially engaged Bible reading. By now internationally renowned, CBS purposely aims for justice with real impact in real-life settings. Southern African Bible scholars—such as Masenya and Nadar—have promoted gender activism in their scholarship. In Botswana, too, such activist-purposed readings are emerging, and I examined some of these by Dube, Berman, Gabaitse, and myself. What follows, builds on this foundation. Following Dube's work at the height of the HIV and AIDS pandemic, I am first, targeting my Bible reading towards naming and confronting a current crisis (in my case gender-based violence [GBV]), and second, I am inter-reading biblical texts with real-life events in Botswana.[1] The Bible is widely accepted in Botswana as the word and book of God; I want to show that it is also a Batswana book. Yes, it contains dreadful stories of GBV that reflect dreadful events happening in Botswana. Rather than accepting this as "just how it is and will always be," it can give us the words to name GBV and the tools to go beyond recognition and confront GBV. As God's word and *our* word, we can and must choose to read the Bible for our liberation from GBV. To this I turn next.

Reading the Bible as a Motswana woman, I am confronted by its patriarchal mores and stories, which resonate with what I see in my own setting. The Bible's saturation with hegemonic masculinity, male chauvinism, and misogynistic attitudes detrimentally impacts the female characters in biblical stories. This, to me now, is glaring in the texts, and the similarities with the context in which I live do not escape me. And yet, I am embarrassed to admit that even though I grew up in church, attending religiously from a young age, and studied at a Christian mission boarding school for five years of high school, with the Bible a constant presence and influence on my life, it was only when training as a biblical scholar, much later in my life, that I came to recognize the endemic presence of violence, including GBV, in biblical stories. Though the Bible was read in church and at school assemblies every morning, it was always *nice* stories, or so we (my peers and I) were led to believe. That is partly what influenced my love for the Bible and its God. Those who stood before me during those seminal years made me think about the Bible as a "good book" and to see the Bible, its people, their God, and all its stories as a kind of paradise world to be envied, earned, and finally adopted through believing in its God. It was a world beyond criticism.

Somehow, much of what was undeniably there, in the Bible, became unseen. I was somehow not struck by or pondering about Dinah, or David's daughter Tamar, or the Levite's wife. Nor was I encouraged to ponder on their stories. These stories became hidden in plain sight, made invisible. And I wonder now that what they depict—GBV and sexual violence—consequently became normalized, and ignored, by me and by others, in the biblical text and also in the world in which I was experiencing the Bible. Meanwhile, other texts, "nicer" texts, loomed much larger, creating a kind of smokescreen. Believing in the God of the Bible meant to belong, to be chosen; as stated in Galatians 3:28, it meant that "There is neither Jew nor Gentile, neither slave nor free, nor is there male or female, for you are all one in Christ." The emphasis, as I recall it, always fell on the first part "neither Jew nor Gentile." Although the text could be used as a liberating one for gender justice, too, that did not seem to be the primary agenda. What was emphasized was to be chosen (like the Jewish people in the first testament) —but hierarchies quietly remained: There were still maids and masters in the world I lived in, and there were also gendered hierarchies. Just like the stories of GBV in the Bible, these other persistent inequalities named in the Galatians verse remained, if mostly unchallenged and unseen. The oneness in Christ was not and often is still not pushing against class and gender injustices, which, in Botswana, often intersect.[2] For instance, the United Nations Development Program (UNDP), Botswana reports the prevailing socio-economic gender inequality as follows:

> Female participation in the labour force is uneven – 56.5% of women and 64.6% of men – with a higher unemployment rate among women (23.5%) relative to men (21.7%). The persistence of the gender pay gap may be explained by segregation of women into lower-paid and low-value sectors of the labour market. While the distribution of public officials is gender balanced, males overrepresent in key ministries, and the percentage of men earning at the highest pay-scale is significantly higher than women.
> (UNDP, Botswana 2021: 6)[3]

The point I want to bring home is that the Bible was presented to me from a young age as a beautiful gateway to humanity's final destination: To heaven, over against its antithesis, hell. I loved Bible stories and regarded them as salvation dramas about the mighty acts of God saving his *chosen* people, namely, the Israelites but also, by extension, my people and me. Nobody during those formative years of my life drew my attention to any problematic features and contents of biblical texts or to the world that produced them and the world these stories reflect (arguably, right up to the present). I learned to read and interpret selectively and also to unsee and ignore large parts of the Bible, to accept it in a particular way, and not to critique it. For me, reflecting back, this contributes towards explaining why in my contemporary context, too, acts of GBV, not dissimilar to those routinely passed over in biblical texts, are rampant—despite the presence of and adherence to the "good bits" of the Bible. Maybe, if we can learn to see, critique, and call out GBV in the Bible, we can also do better at seeing, calling out, and resisting GBV in our midst.

Today, I still wonder what was wrong with my teachers, my pastors, and chaplains: How did they manage to miss or conceal the violence, chaos, and rottenness so rampant in the Bible? How could they not direct us towards seeing and thinking through the portrayals of biblical heroes and even of God as tyrants, racists, misogynists, and insecure patriarchs? I recollect that if some not-so-perfect characters or events were ever mentioned, which happened relatively rarely, such were either explained as consequences of human sin, or as the work of the devil, with no further examination. How could we have been taught so successfully to read past stories of GBV, while GBV was happening all around us? Up until today, it is still rare, certainly in Botswana, to hear the biblical narratives of GBV read from church pulpits. Instead, these texts remain in a kind of limbo: They are in the Bible, which is sacred and "good," but they are not discussed, let alone interrogated. And this is reminiscent of the presence of GBV in Botswana, which persists and shows no sign of abating, but which is also not being confronted and interrogated—or, when it is, not adequately or effectively. The observable trend, in my context, is selective biblical readings that aim not to disturb the status quo of male supremacy, female subordination, and heteronormativity.[4]

While it is possible to choose many more examples from the Bible, in this chapter I explore four biblical narratives relevant to the topic of male-female dynamics and GBV: The creation stories of Genesis 1–3, the rape narrative of Tamar in 2 Samuel 13, the characterizations of Vashti and Esther in the book of Esther, and the brutal treatment of the Levite's concubine in Judges 19.[5] As I will demonstrate, all of these have resonance with events in contemporary Botswana and I will inter-read the biblical texts with reports in the country's national newspapers, namely *The Botswana Daily News*, *Mmegi*, *The Sunday Standard*, *The Voice*, and *The Botswana Gazette*. The selection of biblical texts is intended to frame and to focus a bigger discussion. The texts from the Bible and newspapers do not represent the whole picture of GBV in either the Bible or Botswana society—but they may bring us closer to confronting both.

I will show how biblical texts and contemporary events point to violence against women and explore how religious authorities, sometimes in collusion with traditional culture, have done too little to challenge a status quo where GBV-supportive attitudes and rape culture persist. This, in turn, has seen women ravaged, broken, lost, killed, buried, silenced, and forgotten, together with their legacies, just like the women of the Bible whose stories we will explore in this chapter. But I will also argue that biblical texts are dynamic and lend themselves to multiple interpretations. The starting point toward achieving the transformative ability of biblical texts is first to examine and confront them.

Once we have come to terms with the realities of violence against women in the Bible, I believe we will see more clearly the harm perpetrated against women in our present times. As observed by Johanna Stiebert, since the Bible continues to exert influence into the present, the erasure of rape and, indeed, any form of violence, from the biblical text, can enable, even legitimate, the persistence of similar acts in contemporary societies (Stiebert 2020, 7). But uncovering, calling out, and critically analyzing acts of violence in biblical narratives might also act as a wake-up call and as a disruptor to the realities of violence against women in contemporary contexts. From there, the Bible might guide us onwards, from *acknowledging* violence perpetrated against women and girls since ancient times to *redirecting* us towards activism to confront and prevent GBV. That way we might break toxic patterns in gender relations.

I will begin with the story of the creation of human beings as differently sexed bodies and how the biblical account, right from the start, presents readers with not just conflicting accounts but also an ambiguous presentation of the female-sexed body. The harmful legacy of interpreting this text against women has sadly stood the test of time.

Genesis 1–3: The Beginning of Deposition of Females—and of GBV

In the story of creation recorded in Genesis 1 and 2, we read about how humanity came into being just after the Earth and everything in it. In Genesis 3, we reach a breaking point in which males and females, initially *presumed* equals, in harmony with the grand plan of creation, lose the equilibrium of equality. Initially, the narrative of human creation states this:

> So, God created humankind in his image, in the image of God he created them; male and female he created them.
> (Genesis 1:27)

This verse implies that males and females (and possibly other sexes too)[6] are divinely co-created, which might well imply an absence of hierarchy.

There is certainly no explicit suggestion of hierarchy, division, or rank. However, in Genesis 2:21–23, the situation could be seen to shift.

So, the Lord God caused the man to fall into a deep sleep; while he was sleeping, he took one of the man's ribs and then closed the place with flesh. Then God made a woman from the rib he had taken out of the man, and he brought her to the man.

The usual trend in Botswana settings is that Genesis 1:27 is sublimated, while the latter account in Genesis 2 is amplified. And here the male is created first, which is interpreted as indicative of precedence and pre-eminence (Stanton, 1985). Indeed, in Genesis 1, the woman is "dignified as an important factor in creation, equal in power and glory with man" (Clines 1990, 3). The contrasting stories regarding the creation of the female (whether simultaneously *with* the male or later, and derivatively, *from* his rib) have been debated by feminist scholars for over a century. Elizabeth Stanton blames the skewed emphasis on what she suspects to be some "wily writer, who seeing that man and woman in the first chapter of Genesis, were perfectly equal mates, decided to change the story (in Gen 2) in favour of the dignity and supremacy of man to effect woman's subordination" (Clines 1990, 3). As though that was not enough, Genesis 3 pushes the agenda of inequality yet further: Here the woman is subordinated, and becomes entirely marginalized, losing her earlier agency. Woman, Eve, becomes the one who fell into temptation first, disobeys God first, and *causes* the man to disobey God, too. It is stated thus:

When the woman saw that the fruit was good for food and pleasing to the eye, and also desirable for gaining wisdom, she took some and ate it. She also gave some to her husband, who was with her, and he ate it.

(Genesis 3:6)

For the disobedience that the couple committed, God issues punishments and a curse for all involved: The serpent, who tricked the woman; the woman herself; and the man. Also cursed, alongside the serpent (3:14), is the earth (3:17), which has not done any wrong. However, the punishment upon the woman (widely called a curse in my Botswana context, contrary to the text), part of which is "… your desire will be for your husband, and he will rule over you" (Genesis 3:16b), has taken precedence in interpretation, justifying the subordination of women to men to this day. Genesis 3:16, together with Genesis 2:21, has functioned as a tool for implementing and legitimating gender inequality to the detriment of women. The same has in my view contributed to the ever-growing pandemic of violence against women and girls. This is because of the correlation between gendered inequality and abuse of power, where those more powerful (mostly men) abuse those less powerful (mostly women). Having a foundational sacred text (such as Genesis 3, for instance) that appears to support this inequality, moreover, serves to legitimate, even prescribe its exploitative consequences. Notably, the woman's punishment sexualizes her: She is desirous; her (sexual) desire for men is divinely mandated. This is easy to interpret—as it often is in my context—as the woman being about and for sex. Again, this has had dire impact, with sexual assault of women often being treated casually: For instance, in terms of women "asking for it" or men having a right to expect sex from women.

Genesis 1–3 has impacted many cultures and communities across the world where the Bible has reach, supporting patriarchy and its strategies of domination, marginalization, and violence—not just over women but other vulnerable groups, too, including children, sexual minorities, and those with disabilities. The patriarchal ideologies of the Bible have also been used in partnership and collusion with patriarchal cultures, including the Setswana culture, to oppress women and suffocate their dreams of fulfilment, curtailing their freedom to live to their full potential. This will be explored further as this chapter unfolds. In my context, many women have lost their lives at the hands of men because not only are women in Botswana treated as inferior to males but it is as if their lives matter less. Why else are women killed with such alarming regularity by their current or ex-husbands, lovers, and, less often, strangers? For instance, one study done in Botswana, which relied on the country's newspapers, indicates that "From 2003 to 2012, 747 people were murdered by those who claimed to love them. Of this total number, female victims accounted for the largest number of victims, with 689 cases compared to 57 men" (Bagai and Faimau 2021). No wonder, the Botswana Daily News recently had the title "Botswana Still Safe for Women," a title which though appears to be affirmative is in essence either a rhetorical question or a sarcastic statement as the contents therein point to the ever-growing desperation regarding incidences of GBV against women in Botswana.[7]

I want to take a few steps back to explore further the creation account of Genesis 1–3. I want to demonstrate how Eve's legacy has influenced or colluded with Botswana's patriarchal culture to the detriment of Batswana women. I will do this as an introduction to the general depiction and subordination of women both in the Bible and in my context—Botswana. The analysis will mainly serve as a background to the inter-reading of biblical stories of GBV against women in the selected texts and stories of GBV against Batswana women.

Eve and GBV: The Embodiment of a *Fallen*[8] Model for All Women

An Archetype

As noted by Carolyn Curtis James, whose sentiments I share, "before we attempt to understand any other women in the Bible, much less ourselves, we have the important groundwork to do with Eve, for she is the foundation of all that follows" (James 2005, 30). This projects some sense of the tremendous importance accorded to the story in Genesis 2–3 and to the impact of Eve for women subsequently—in particular, for women living and growing up in settings where the Bible holds authority and importance—as is the case with me. The common interpretation of Eve accounts for the woman's existence as fulfilling the man's need: She exists because of him and to satisfy him, but she is subordinate in status to him (Alter 1980, 146). She has suffered centuries of being portrayed as the weaker of two human creatures and as the one who disobeyed God first. Sometimes she is depicted as a temptress or trickster who led the man, Adam, into disobedience by offering him the forbidden fruit. Hence, Eve has come to represent weakness, fatal attraction, and fallenness; following her model, while women after Eve may have their uses, they must be dominated and controlled to punish past wrongdoing and to prevent future potential dangers to which, by implication, women, like Eve before them, are predisposed. Indeed, what Paul does with Genesis 2 and 3 in the New Testament is testimony that this particular understanding, or misunderstanding, of Eve has extensive ramifications for females long after. He writes in an oft-cited text, very familiar to churchgoers in Botswana, that is now canonical for Christians:

> A woman should learn in quietness and full submission. I do not permit a woman to teach or to assume authority over a man; she must be quiet, for Adam was formed first, then Eve. And Adam was not the one deceived; it was the woman who was deceived and became a sinner.
> (1 Tim. 2: 11–14)

> Women should remain silent in the churches. They are not allowed to speak but must be in submission, as the law says. If they want to inquire about something, they should ask their husbands at home; for it is disgraceful for women to speak in the church.
> (1 Cor. 14: 34–35)

Anecdotally, Christian women seeking help from the church regarding intimate partner violence (IPV) have been discouraged and even prevented from quitting violent relationships or marriages, with such passages from the Bible widely pointed to. Biblical texts that have been used to challenge women enduring and reporting IPV include the ones above as well as Matthew 18: 21–22 (urging forgiveness up to 77 times), Ephesians 5:22-and Colossians 3:18 (stressing wives' submission to their husbands; see Marsden 2018, 12).

I can attest to the damaging effects of biblical texts such as these from personal experience. Coupled with the construction of Eve as sexualized and sinful, such interpretations continue to infuse and shape gender relations, with destructive results for women. Sadly, some Christian women in abusive and violent marriages and relationships choose to endure and stay for the same reasons as those given by their abusers (Marsden 2018). In my context of Botswana, such damaging biblical interpretations are further reinforced by Setswana patriarchal culture to subordinate women to the rule of men, including bowing to IPV. For instance, in Setswana culture and tradition, as already discussed, women are called "cows"[9] and must remain on the peripheries of society, as wives, mothers, and caregivers. In contrast, leadership positions remain traditionally reserved for men (who are likened to more powerful "bulls"). Traditional laws and power relations were and remain skewed along gendered lines. According to Nkomazana, missionaries to Botswana were quick to endorse the indigenous patriarchal status quo, strategically affirming it with appropriate biblical proof-texts (Nkomazana 2008, 83). But the idea of the *fallen* woman of Genesis, or the subservient wife of Ephesians, is not a new or foreign one to Batswana and is captured in Setswana idioms and proverbs such as *Ga nke di etelelwa pele ke manamagadi*, literally, "Cows can never lead the herd." Here again, women are viewed as depicted as inherently weak, unsuitable for, and incapable of leadership (Bauer 2010). Genesis 1–3 landed on fertile ground in Botswana. This shows once more that biblical and Setswana patriarchies met and merged with devastating consequences and with impact right up to present-day life in Botswana (Togarasei 2016). Yet Eve has also been the subject of feminist biblical scholarship spanning many, many decades,[10] and some of this not only identifies how biblical texts can propel harm but also how they can present us with positive role models.

The country's newspaper headlines point to the graveness of such incidences even though they, too, "do not represent female victims of intimate partner homicides (IPH) fairly as they maintain denigration, degradation, and infantilization of women in their reports" (Bagai and Faimau 2021). The stories will be analyzed in what follows.

Grabbing of Vaginas:[11] 2 Samuel 13 and Rape Narratives from Botswana

Before proceeding with my analysis, it is important to stress that child sexual abuse, including incestuous child abuse, is also, like GBV and other forms of sexual abuse, a global and under-reported problem causing devastating harm. Data from separate countries tends to be patchy and is more reliable in some places than others (see Shumba and Moorad 2000; Singh, Parsekar and Nair 2014 *passim*). Indeed, sexual violence may be perpetrated by as well as against men, women, boys, and girls. Where data exists, however, victims are predominantly female and perpetrators, overwhelmingly, are male. This is reflected also regarding sexual abuse in the Bible (see Stiebert 2020, *passim*). Sexual abuse, therefore, is gendered, and this applies also to child sexual abuse and incestuous abuse of children wherever data is available.

In 2 Samuel 13, a girl-child is overpowered and raped by her older brother. The rape happens in the royal house of King David and the rapist is his eldest son, Amnon. The victim is David's daughter, Amnon's half-sister, Tamar. She is a virgin and, in all likelihood, given what is suspected about marriage practices in ancient Israel, young. The text depicts Amnon's actions in stark terms, as follows:

> … he grabbed her …
>
> (v. 11)
>
> … he raped her …
>
> (v. 14)
>
> … he hated her …
>
> (v. 15)

and

> he commanded his servant to get her out of his sight and bolt the door after her, and he obeyed.
>
> (vv. 17–18)

The rape happens in the company of other men, who, in my opinion, are not innocent. They collude that Jonadab, King David, and Amnon's unnamed personal servant are all players in the drama and their roles make them partners in Amnon's crime. It is no wonder that Thiede concludes that in the narratives of the book of Samuel the ideal man is the one who engages in sexual violence, raping women, and exerting his dominance over other lesser men who become partners, bystanders, or witnesses to the sexual violence performed by *their hero* (Thiede 2022, 22). What happens to Tamar in 2 Samuel 13 fits perfectly into the structure described by Thiede. Tamar is raped by one powerful man (the royal firstborn), but the conspirators in the "game" are multiple and they together ensure that the act of sexual violence is planned and carried out against her. Amnon is the man who is supported by other males to rape Tamar. Perhaps, these men gain Amnon's favor in this way? Perhaps they derive voyeuristic delight in their collusion? At any rate, they are complicit. As Thiede demonstrates, hegemonic masculinity is systemic and endemic in biblical texts. It operates as a chain of command, involving many players who help to sustain and maintain its goals. Rape violates even a royal daughter who is described as innocent—the text describes her as a virgin (v. 11) and as vocally resisting Amnon's violence (2 Sam. 13: 12–13). Still, Tamar is entrapped, surrounded by a bunch of fully grown men, who seal her fate. They all work together to deliver her up like a lamb to the slaughter. Their plan succeeds as her body is ravaged and then disposed of.

The narrative of Tamar displays a patriarchal, misogynistic world infested with GBV, a world in which males (boys and men) rule while females (women and girls) who are reduced to commodities and objects. The typical hegemonic masculinity that allows male domination over women plays out in the story about Tamar's rape (Connell 2005, 77 cited by Thiede 2022 22). Decisions are made for her by the men in the story. She is ordered and told what to do, and there is no indication that she has any option but to obey the men's commands. First, her father, David, who is supposedly her number-one-protector, prefers to satisfy his son Amnon's desire to have Tamar go to serve him food in his private chamber, without thinking twice about any possible risks that might compromise his young daughter's safety. Perhaps he knew what would happen;[12] at any rate, after the rape, he is no more than angry, taking no action. This story is about men and their selfish needs. Jonadab, another male chauvinist, plays the role of fixer, who devises the plan to satisfy another man's, Amnon's, desire to get whatever he wants from Tamar; after all, she is a girl and beautiful (i.e., in the toxic hegemonic masculine mindset, "made for sex"). It is clear what Amnon wants to do with Tamar as he expresses it to Jonadab, whom the text describes as "shrewd" (2 Samuel 13: 3). Jonadab comes up with a clever plan to get Tamar to the *slaughter* table where her vagina will be *grabbed* (v. 11), used, and cast out (vv. 14, 15, and 17). As if that is not enough, another male character, Amnon's servant, takes up the finishing baton to dispose of Tamar (v. 17). As maintained by Barbra Thiede (2022), men in this story actively collude and plan together, sharing mental images of the woman's body. Unambiguously, what happens to Tamar is sexual violence; it is rape, one of multiple horrific forms of GBV. It immediately reminds me of the many similar crimes against Batswana girls. I will turn to some of the stories reported in our newspapers, echoed in and by Tamar's story.

Tales like Tamar's, where rape involves powerful men, with important roles and standing in their society, covering for one another, of rape perpetrated against helpless minor girls, are familiar also from my context. Children cannot protect themselves against adults and are particularly helpless in the face of power. Abuse of minors is termed "defilement" in the Botswana Penal Code, which indeed echoes the language applied to the rape of both Dinah (Genesis 34:2, 5, 7, 13, and 27) and Tamar (2 Samuel 13:12–13, 16, 22, and 32).

The law of defilement (Section 147) states that "intercourse with a child under the age of 16 years constitutes an offense." The law was revised in 2018 to increase the age of consent to 18 years (Shumba and Moorad 2000, 175).[13] The offense of defilement is punishable by law with a minimum of ten years or a maximum of life imprisonment. Sadly, in spite of the existence of this law, it is no strong deterrent, and there are many occurrences of defilement in Botswana, most often perpetrated against girl-children, including by highly respected male members of the society. Sometimes such defilement is incestuous, perpetrated by girls' fathers, stepfathers, uncles, or older brothers (like Amnon). Most often defilement is committed by entitled and powerful men with leadership positions in society (like both Amnon and David). It is also disheartening, alongside the rate at which men molest children, how law enforcement agencies reportedly regularly display reluctance or indifference towards such incidences. As in the biblical story, it is men who dominate the law enforcement sector, and who actively and passively facilitate defilement. We shall next examine some of the many cases reported in Botswana's national newspapers.

This is a headline you don't want to see: "Botswana Records Largest Increase in Defilement Cases" (Mokwape 2021). According to the *Mmegi* newspaper report, during the COVID-19 lockdown, Botswana recorded the country's highest number of GBV-related cases, including child sexual molestation or defilement.[14] Statistics from the Botswana Police Service note an increase in reported defilement cases from 1,208 cases in 2019 to 1,825 in 2020.[15] These statistics are particularly chilling, given that it is known of such crimes that unreported cases tend to far outnumber reported ones. Reasons for low reporting rates include but are not limited to victims' and witnesses' fear of retribution by perpetrators, dependency and the fear that perpetrators may lose their jobs and be unable to support victims under their care, and shame and being seen as causing community discord.[16] In Botswana, the predominant culture teaches children to be respectful of and submissive to adults, and taboos concerning sexual matters are powerful, both of which contribute to vulnerability to sexual abuse of children, as well as to under-reporting. As a result, statistics for reported defilement cases are considerably lower than those of teenage pregnancy in the country, which frequently include low-age teenage pregnancy (Ramabu 2020).

The UNICEF interim report reflecting on the COVID-19 pandemic (2020) also substantiates reasons for grave concern. Shockingly and distressingly, the youngest rape victim recorded here is only two years old.[17] A summative Botswana Police Service report reveals that between 2019 and 2021, 5,000 girl-children were raped in Botswana. The report further indicates that in 2021 alone, 2,003 cases of child sexual molestation and rape were recorded and that the primary perpetrators were fathers, stepfathers, brothers, and cousins.[18] These statistics shed some light on the rampancy of GBV, including the widespread sexual violence suffered by Batswana girl-children. The fact that perpetrators are often close family members again recalls the ordeal of biblical Tamar's rape. Girl children's bodies are snatched and abused, including by male family members who are supposed to be their protectors, according to both biblical culture and Setswana culture. Cultural mores and jurisdictions neither have protected Botswana's children. And every single victim represents a body, mind, and soul deeply and profoundly harmed and represents broken trust, dreams, and stifled fulfilment.

One paper headline reads, "Father Defiles Teen Daughter"[19] (Moemedi 2022). In this Voice newspaper article, it states that a 45-year father raped his 12-year-old daughter on several occasions, sometimes in the presence of the girl's mother, and multiple occurrences went unreported to the police.[20] This indicates the abuse the mother and the daughter were subjected to. It is not a surprise that the case went unreported for a long time, given some of the reasons discussed already that make reporting such cases difficult for the victims as well as the witnesses. In GBV-infested homes, such as the one in question, the mother and her children exist under the tyrannical rule of the man, whom society views as the head of the house. He demonstrates a sense of dominance, ownership, and control, especially over the females under his thumb, and he uses sexual violence to exert overall power.

The Voice newspaper headline reads "BDP Councillor in Hot Soup for Defilement" (Botlhoko 2021). This case reveals how a politician of the ruling Botswana Democratic Party (BDP), a political district councillor, was charged with defiling a 16-year-old minor whom he impregnated.[21] This is far from a singular case of abuse of power. There is evidence that female bodies, whether of women or girls, are regularly viewed by Batswana males (boys and men) as sexual objects for the gratification of their sexual desire. Such a view and entitlement mentality have led to the steeply rising cases of reported GBV in all its horrific forms, all to the detriment of women and girls in the country. It does not matter whether one is a child, married, or unmarried; if one has a vagina, one is deemed usable and disposable by entitled males. Indeed, the same can be said about some biblical narratives, like that of 2 Samuel 13.

No wonder church leaders, too, who are, again, predominantly men, have also committed horrendous acts of violence against women. Let me cite three recent cases from Botswana:

- "SDA Pastor Back in Court for Sex Worker's Murder" (Baaitse 2023). The Voice newspaper report details how a Seventh Day Adventist Church pastor in Botswana solicited the services of a Zimbabwean sex worker and spent the night at her place before running off the next morning when a friend of the sex worker came to visit. She found her friend lying naked and dead on the floor with used condoms nearby."[22]
- "Unholy Horror: Apostle Accused of Raping Teen in Church Toilet" (Mlilo 2023). It is purported that a 17-year-old girl was raped in the church toilets by a church leader, an Apostle of a new charismatic movement, during a church service.[23]
- "Major Kills Private, Turns Rifle on Himself" (*Mmegi*, Staff Writer 2022). The Botswana Defence Force boss, holding the position of Major, who was also reported to be a church minister, medical doctor, and a married man, killed his girlfriend, a female member of the Defence Force, during a deployment mission in Mozambique.[24] Further investigations revealed that the killer suspected that his girlfriend was cheating on him.[25] This is an example of a crime called a "passion killing" in Botswana.

The above stories from Botswana newspapers provide a sample and emphasize the point that even though the Bible is a respected text in Botswana, this does not restrain or limit those who proclaim it every Sunday, standing at the pulpit in front of Bible-believing congregations, reading its stories, and interpreting them for the church congregants, from committing acts of violence. GBV, above all against female folk, including young girls, happens in the church and is committed and covered up by men who exploit their power (be this their power as fathers, politicians, or church leaders). And these, moreover, are men knowledgeable about the biblical text.

Arguably, following Thiede (2022, *passim*), some biblical texts actually *teach* rape culture. Not only are there many biblical texts depicting GBV, in which women are treated as trash, traditional Setswana culture supplements such violence, and the consequences, played out on women's and girls' raped and murdered bodies, bear testimony to this. Importantly, the point I want to drive home is that there is urgent need for alternative and liberationist ways of reading biblical texts such as the Tamar' story. And in this book, I suggest that naming and confronting such texts (as 2 Sam. 13) can be reparative and that readers must also acknowledge that biblical narratives reflect real life as we know and experience it in our contemporary world. As we have seen in the preceding discussion with examples from the Botswana context, the resonance between what happens to biblical women and girls (done almost exclusively by men and boys) and what happens to Botswana girls and women is overwhelming and shows that the world presented in these texts, though ancient as they may be, is no different from our own-contemporary world. Therefore, the Tamar Campaign found in South Africa and Kenya, which I discussed in the previous chapter, uses this story and this can be adapted for Botswana context. As a way of naming the GBV—in this case the rape of a biblical textual girl, named Tamar, schoolgirls in Botswana could learn that suffering abuse (as rape, etc.) is not their fault just as it is clearly not Tamar's fault. The book of Esther bears further witnesses to the claims I am making here.

The Book of Esther and GBV in Botswana: Silencing, Barred Choices, and Banishments

Reading the Book of Esther, one is confronted by the display of the *rotten* power of "King Xerxes who ruled over 127 provinces stretching from India to Cush" (Est. 1:1–8). Notable too about this story is that there are countless women, most of them nameless, except for three, two of whom are our focus here: Vashti and Esther, who live under the tyrannical rule of the King and his multiple councillors and advisers, including eunuchs.[26] As observed by Randall Bailey, "The book of Esther is fraught with problems and tensions" (Bailey 2020, 167). My interest is in the GBV that abounds in the narrative, including the sex trafficking of girls (Dunbar 2021). In Esther 1 and 2, there is a casual description of what would have been horrific experiences of violence for the women taken from their homes to "please" the King.[27] The King is the highest authority in the empire, delegating to his council of servants, eunuchs, and all other men who, as the text reveals, have power over their own wives

(Estther 1: 20). As observed by Ericka Dunbar (2021), in traditional Esther readings and discourses, recourse to comedy genres often downplays the violent nature of this text and distracts readers away from such elements.

When reading the book of Esther as a Motswana woman who lives and works in Botswana, I feel some affinity with the characters of Esther and Vashti. Both the book and my cultural context are rape cultures, where violence is normalized, and women are told not to "make a fuss." Both the book and my cultural context relegate women to roles where they are subject to men's control and socialized to please men, through being attractive and submissive to men. Both the book and my cultural context render the vast bulk of GBV (in the book, the mass rape of the nameless virgins from all across the empire) invisible and insignificant. I feel for Vashti when she refuses to parade, possibly naked but for a royal diadem, in front of a room full of drunken dignitaries who have been drinking without limit for 180 days (Est. 1: 8, 12). For me, this echoes the abuses of women in Botswana who are subjected to sexual harassment and ostracized for refusing their male associates' abusive demands: Whether sexual, economic, domestic, etc. We, too, like Vashti, often have no acceptable choices or alternatives, and if we dare refuse, we can suffer banishment, isolation, and worse. This is not from the palace, like Vashti, but from our homes, jobs, careers, and sometimes from life itself in the form of femicide.

Newspaper headlines declaring violence are commonplace in Botswana and seem to increase yearly. One of these is, "Crimes of Passion: National Crises,"[28] and its attendant article relates how Botswana is riddled with cases of female murders resulting from "love" relationships and dubbed "passion killings." During the country's one-day Independence Day celebration, which takes place annually on September 30, 12 murder cases were reported to the Botswana police service. In all 12 cases, the victims were women, and the perpetrators were men.[29] Research shows that such homicides occur when a woman, often following abuse, wants or tries to end a relationship with a man (Exner and Thurston 2009; Mookodi 2004; Raditloaneng 2013). In such instances, as in the Vashti ordeal, the woman is expected to bow to the man's demands, to obey whatever instruction, no matter how demeaning, with failure to do so resulting in great risk. Vashti was banished from her husband King Xerxes's presence, as we imagine her dragged out by the king's servants and forever forfeiting the luxuries as queen and her friends in the royal palace (Kebaneilwe 2011). With her banishment, Vashti disappears from the story. She is silenced, like so many girls and women in Botswana.

One of the many heart-wrenching stories of homicide in Botswana was titled "The Family of Murdered Teacher Speaks Out."[30] According to the *Mmegi* newspaper report, the female teacher, aged 48 years, was murdered by two hitmen hired by her estranged husband. According to the victim's brother, the brutal incident happened while the couple was going through a divorce, and their case had stalled for a long time due to the husband's lack of cooperation. The woman is said to have initiated and registered the divorce with the court. According to further investigations, which at the time of writing this book are still ongoing, the incident happened at night. The slain woman was sleeping with her 6-year-old child (a girl), who is said to have witnessed the gruesome incident during which her mother was sexually assaulted before being murdered.[31] It is entirely plausible that the victim's choice to initiate divorce was motivated by abuse and suffering at the hands of her violent husband and that her decision to leave him led directly to her gruesome assault and murder.

With many so-called passion killings in Botswana, women die because men's egos are bruised when women assert themselves as people who decide what is good and acceptable to them. Vashti is banished and suffers narrative death for similar reasons. Women's abuse happens through and in the presence of men. As noted in the case of Tamar in 2 Samuel 13, men work together in a supply-chain-like manner to carry out abuse and violence against women. In the case of Vashti, her number-one-protector, namely her husband Xerxes, fails to protect her (much like David in Tamar's story fails to protect his daughter), and the slain Botswana teacher's husband also fails in his role of protector to both his child and his child's mother.[32] The resonance is marked.

It goes without saying that if women's choices contradict the desires of the men in their lives, women in both contexts are liable to face terror. Amnon desires Tamar and, when she resists his verbal command, he rapes her; Vashti refuses to be leered at and is banished. In Botswana, overwhelmingly, victims of passion killings are women. As discussed earlier in Chapter 2, Batswana women have suffered in many ways. During the HIV/AIDS pandemic, before the discovery of antiretroviral treatments, many women (even more women than men) succumbed to the virus, often because they were denied choices and decisions in sexual matters, including their right to negotiate safe sex (Dube 2003, 91). This, as noted before, was exacerbated by the silencing tendencies of Botswana culture, which stifles women's ability to seek assistance in cases of abuse by their husbands. Batswana women are disadvantaged as they are taught, told, and expected to be selfless and keep silent about any pain or abuse, especially if it is perpetrated by their spouses in marriage (Ellece 2011, 47; Kebaneilwe 2011, 380). This includes putting up with their husbands' sexual promiscuity, as the culture tolerates such from men but shuns it from women (Dube 2003). Thus, Setswana marriage encourages and orientates women to become "marital fools" (Ellece, 2011,47) whose rights cease and devolve to their husbands. As a result, many women, especially married ones, have died from HIV and AIDS until medication became freely available as it is in Botswana today. Yet still, many today continue getting infected through their husbands or lovers, even when they are submissive and faithful.[33] As with Tamar, being innocent does not protect from harm.

As demonstrated, Vashti's sexualization and, on standing up for herself, her silencing by her husband, King Xerxes, echo the experiences of real, flesh-and-blood Batswana women to this day. If they dare, they may get eliminated; hence, many stay in dysfunctional, abusive marriages and relationships, opting for silence and submissive conformity to cultural expectations, not unlike Queen Esther, who succeeds Vashti. The situation resembles the verdict that was passed following and because of Vashti's refusal to obey the demeaning demands of her husband: An imperial edict ordered *all* women, throughout the 127 provinces of Persia, to be subject to their husbands and never to dare imitate Vashti's actions (Est. 1:16–17). Just as we saw how the figure of Eve was used to confine and restrict *all* women after her, so Vashti becomes the reason for women's generalized subservience. In both cases, this is unfair and unjust and has terrible consequence.[34] This validates male dominance over women and stifles women's assertive actions, promoting that they should be docile in the face of abuses, which is reinforced by fear of victimization and possible ostracization. By analogy, Batswana women, though no written edicts bar them from being proactive in defending their rights and ending abusive relationships, are still, through the canonized and normative texts of the Bible, being signaled to remain compliant. The Bible is used to affirm men and boys as masters over women and girls, whether they are married or unmarried, intimate or strangers; it is also used to affirm women and girls' submission to all men and boys' demands.

Arguably, Vashti, whom some feminist commentators have claimed as a heroic defier of the patriarchy, might also be seen as a role model who dares to resist abuse and chooses to defend her dignity (Kebaneilwe, 2011, 2012). Some brave Batswana women also risk their personal safety and lives by resisting abuse—but Vashti demonstrates that the price to pay can be considerable.

Back to the Esther narrative, it is important to note that Esther, too, was a victim of GBV, much like her predecessor, Vashti, and all the women in King Xerxes' harem and wider territory. We will now look more closely at how GBV unfolds in the treatment of Esther as the Queen of Persia after Vashti.

Objectification and Sexualization: Female Bodies for Male Desire and Gratification

The eponymous female character Esther also reveals how patriarchal attitudes and treatment of women and girls make them objects, particularly of men's sexual desire and gratification. After Vashti's banishment and textual death, a replacement is sought—as women may be pesky and disposable, but they play a necessary role in the patriarchal scheme, as objects to control and to gratify male egos and male demands.

In Esther 2:2, the text explains that all the king's servants raided the entire span of 127 provinces, seeking young, beautiful virgin girls for the king. I imagine them raiding every home and taking whichever girls they deem sexually attractive, without regard for the girls or for their parents, guardians, families, and communities. This is where trauma, both for the victims and their collectives, would result, as expounded by Dunbar (2021). Such daylight abduction of young girls is unsurprising, given the earlier edict that legalizes the absolute rule of men over women and girls, with the King at the top of the hierarchy (Est. 1: 20). The girls are collected like commodities. They are gathered together for a beauty contest, which is more accurately designated a sex contest, or, even more accurately, a rape contest: Whoever would sexually please the king best in a one-night stand would win—but there is no agency or choice or consent on the part of the girls here, just a desperate fight for survival and for some (albeit restricted) quality of life.

Beal (1997, 195), cited by Bailey (2020, 175), explains that in a sexualized political order, beauty and pleasure *serve as* objectification *strategies* (my italics) through which the subjects (i.e., the girls) secure some power. Beauty and sexual gratification dominate King Xerxes' criteria for women in line to be queen, just as he desired that Queen Vashti should parade her beauty and sexual allure in a room full of drunken men for "she was lovely to look at" (Est 1:11). As such, Vashti was a fitting last course (James, 2005, 145). Whereas Vashti resisted and, as a result, was expelled from the palace, Esther and the rest of the girls are forced into the parade, sexually assaulted, and raped by the king so as to have some (minimal) chance of winning the favor of becoming queen. Esther did better than the rest: Her success rests on her physical and sexual beauty, as judged and decided by men in the story. In this she receives some guidance from her guardian, Mordecai, and one of the palace eunuchs. She becomes queen, and this allows her access to luxuries, and indeed to some power—even though her power is limited, as we saw with Vashti, who, though queen, had her power cancelled and her fate determined by men of the palace (Esther 1:16–21).

The story of Esther again echoes some of the difficulties Batswana women and girls negotiate as they navigate their predominately patriarchal culture, systems, and institutions. While the Persian palace and harem have no parallel in Botswana, male exploitation, female beauty, and the expectation that women and girls provide men with sexual pleasure are all too familiar. For instance, in Botswana, youth unemployment has risen for the past decade. Many young men and women struggle to make ends meet (Mogalakwe and Nyamnjoh 2017, 6). One upshot of this has been for older men who hold financially secure or important positions to take advantage of primarily girls seeking some means to survive. This has led to the widespread practice of cross-generational, transactional sexual relationships (Luke and Kurz 2002; Nkosana and Rosenthal 2007 Weiser et al., 2007). In such instances, female physical beauty and sexuality are used as a commodity for men to give desperate women and girls access to money and jobs. As with the girls in the harem, there is no real possibility of consent. The disparity between the parties—older, moneyed men and poor, young women with few opportunities—do not make consent possible. But again, stories like those of Esther normalize and justify such transactional "relationships."

In corrupt, patriarchal systems and institutions, women's education and professional accomplishments can count for little in a difficult job market. As I discuss in more detail elsewhere, earning a living is less about "the certificate and experience and [instead] goes as far as one's underpants" (Kebaneilwe 2018, 60). Such exploitative behavior from men is another form of GBV which dehumanizes women and girls and reduces them to sexual objects. Consequently, the resonance between the treatment of women and girls in the book of Esther and contemporary Batswana women and girls is glaring. In both contexts, women and girls are subjected to multiple forms of GBV. Sadder still, in dire situations, in both the Bible and in Botswana, women and their bodies became spaces of contention, as I shall demonstrate next.

In Dire Situations Women's Bodies Became Spaces of Contention: The Many Faces of GBV in Both the Bible and Botswana

Here is a brief summary of Genesis 19:1–8, a narrative involving Lot and his virgin girls whose bodies became a contentious space in a heinous situation: Two angels arrive in Sodom in the evening, and Lot accommodates them in his house. Later that night, just before going to bed, all the men and boys from the city of Sodom came out to Lot's house demanding to be given the two men (actually, male angels) so they could gang rape them. Lot sees a looming crisis, and, wanting to avert a heinous and wicked thing (v. 7), he instead offers to give his two virgin daughters to "his friends" (as he addresses all the men and the boys) (v. 8). He even tells the congregated males that they could do whatever they wished with his daughters but not to do anything to the male visitors as they had come under his protection.

Lot's actions in response to what he views as a dire situation and crisis, of having his male guests gang raped by the assembled men of Sodom, "old and young," was to offer up his virgin daughters' bodies to be ravaged instead. Notably, this story and the entire Sodom and Gomorrah narrative (Gen. 18–19) have been used to teach and preach against homosexuality. This is common practice in Botswana. Such readings are not only homophobic, but they link homosexuality (an orientation) with violence and with the wrath of God annihilating entire cities (Toensing, 2005, 62). The presence of women and girls and the violence to which they are exposed in the story are often overlooked. According to Katherine Low, Lot's decisions are driven by fear (Low 2010, 39), but in my opinion, based on my experiences as a woman from a GBV-infested context, Lot's decision is also driven by his patriarchal instincts that regard females as lesser persons and, ultimately, as rapable. For him, as is the case in my own context, in a crisis, when men feel helpless and their masculinity challenged, women's bodies serve them to ease their anxieties and to compensate for their feelings of loss of power. Women are there to be treated as objects to serve male's needs and protect male's interests: As Lot puts it, "and you can do as you like with them" (v. 8).

A similar incident happens in the story in Judges 19, where a woman's body (traditionally, she is referred to as the Levite's concubine) is offered up to be raped all night by the men of Gibeah, after they are told they can do whatever they please with her. Again, a woman's body is sacrificed to save men. The implication is that in this biblical world, women are lesser humans to be disposed of as men please.[35] The Levite's concubine, like the host's virgin daughter, who is also offered up (Judg. 19: 25; cf. Gen. 19:8), is treated as a mere object in men's cruel hands. This, in my view, is GBV coupled with misogyny, again, a reality not so far from that suffered by real flesh-and-blood women in Botswana. In the latter part of the story, the man, the Levite in control over the unnamed woman, who is remembered only as his *pilegesh*, sometimes translated "concubine," dismembers her body: "when he reached home, he took a knife and cut up his concubine, limb by limb, into twelve parts ..." (Judg. 19:29).

In my context, some men also do as they like with women's bodies. Consider the following gruesome newspaper headline from Botswana: "Woman Found Beheaded in Tlokweng" (Kgamanyane 2018). In the story reported in *Mmegi* on 30 July 2018, a headless woman's body was found dumped in the bush. A police investigation later revealed that the woman was killed by her intimate partner and that the couple's relationship was characterized by violence and abuse of the deceased by her lover-turned-murderer.[36]

To cite another similar case, "Man Kills Wife at GBV Centre" (Mosolotate 2023). This incident took place in front of a counsellor at a GBV center in Gaborone on 25 May 2023. The woman had gone to seek assistance and mediation at the center, whereupon she met her demise during a counseling session where her husband stabbed her to death. The same report further states that another man accused of murder also appeared before the same Magistrate for murdering his police officer girlfriend.[37] And yet another similar incident was reported the same week, in which an estranged husband murdered his wife, a deputy school head, in cold blood, in an incident reported in an article with the heading, "Man Found Hanging in Police Cells After Killing Wife" (Mlilo 2023).[38] It is reported that after being arrested for killing his wife, the man committed suicide while in police custody. And again, still in the same week (a span of just seven days), in yet another newspaper article, desperately titled "Stop Killing Women" (Mlilo 2023), another woman was murdered in her house by a stranger who was later identified as a 19-year-old boy who had broken into the woman's house that fateful night.[39] The stories cited here are but the tip of the iceberg, and every single one is a tragedy, representing loss of life and potential, with awful repercussions for many loved ones, and striking fear into many more.

In all the cases cited above, the murderers were unemployed men. While unemployment affects both men and women, it is one of multiple contributing factors that exacerbate Batswana men's resentment and anger toward assertive, independent women. As previous studies show, patriarchal culture inculcates men to be not only superior to and controlling of women but also providers and breadwinners for their families (Kebaneilwe, 2011, 2012; Dube 2003). Failure to maintain such culturally determined roles due to unemployment seems to transpire in feelings of inadequacy and castration of manhood, which are then violently "resolved" in the form of GBV, including femicides. Once more women are blamed and women suffer. Women suffer whether they are powerless and submissive and, therefore, easily exploited or whether they are perceived as more successful than men and, therefore, making them feel inadequate.

When situations become dire, through unemployment or other threats, as in the Lot story, too, women regularly become the bearers of hardship and the targets of violence. Unemployment adds to the complex causes of but does not in and of itself account for GBV in Botswana, where women's and girls' lives and bodies have become sites of contention for a range of societal ills. Women bear the bulk of the brunt, be this as victims of the GBV pandemic as of the HIV and AIDS pandemic.[40] During the COVID-19 pandemic, too, cases of GBV in all its forms increased, with particular detriment, once again, to women and girls. As determined by UNICEF Botswana (2022), the pandemic further exacerbated existing and gendered vulnerabilities.[41]

Women's vulnerabilities are multiple. Violence against women is heightened, for instance, during and after war.[42] While Botswana, mercifully, has been spared war in recent years, the country receives asylum seekers escaping war in neighboring countries. Many of them are traumatized rape survivors. Also, drug and alcohol abuse have been linked to the ever-rising GBV incidences in the country, always disproportionately to the detriment of women and girls who are once more the ones most often on the receiving end of physical brutality resulting from substance misuse. For example, the story reported under the heading "Killer Son Found Naked Near Dead Mum"[43] shows how drug and substance abuse by men and boys puts women's and girls' bodies and lives on the line. Drugs and alcohol are used as scapegoats, blamed for leading the abusers to perform horrendous acts. In this story, a 19-year-old boy was found naked and intoxicated in his mother's house, with his mother's naked body lying in a pool of blood.[44] Investigations revealed that the woman had been abused by her own son before the tragic incident and that he had controlled and made her life a living hell. This is one particularly awful case of many where alcohol and drug abuse see women's and girls' bodies mutilated by boys and men.[45] Many of the less unusual cases, where the woman might not be attacked fatally and where her attacker is a more predictable one—such as her boyfriend, or husband—are not even reported. They are, quite simply, not even newsworthy.

As in the Lot story, in times of crisis, be this the COVID-19 pandemic, war, or a domestic crisis, women's bodies become acutely vulnerable and sites of contention. Men and boys "act out their frustrations" on women and girls—it is so commonplace as to be unremarkable (and is often unremarked on or excused). Men and boys turn to use women's bodies as objects on which they take out their anger and frustrations; they break women's bodies to act out their sense of defeat in the face of life's challenges. But this is no justification.

The biblical men, namely Lot, the Levite, and the man who accommodated him, acted similarly. When they felt powerless against a mob of men in the city, they took it out on the women under their care and control, for indeed, Lot effectively owned his daughters as the Levite, apparently, owned his concubine. To hold on to their power or to show off their dominance over the women as their property, they exposed them to other men's violence. Again, there is no justification for this.

It may not be a far-fetched idea to conclude that, as noted throughout this book, the Bible, its narratives, and images have much in common with GBV discourses as described in the patriarchal Botswana context, with women and girls very often falling victim. At the same time, it is men and boys who are most often the perpetrators. We have already seen illustrations of the resonance of biblical stories with real-time, real people's stories from Botswana. The cases cited are just the tip of the iceberg, highlighting fragments of the current GBV crisis. Without offering any quick fix to resolve or eliminate the entrenched and deep-rooted causes of GBV, this book calls with urgency for using the Bible to not only help identify similarities pointing to endemic problems (as in this chapter) but also for social transformation, specifically for addressing GBV. I have shown the influence of the Bible; my purpose will be to apply this influence towards solutions.

Conclusions towards Solutions

In the Hebrew Bible, it is most often men who rule and it is women who are to submit. It all begins with the biblical story of the creation of humankind. Though the story of the creation of humans appears in two dissimilar versions in Genesis 1 and Genesis 2, the second account is all too often given precedence in the history of interpretation.[46] Whereas in Genesis 1, both sexes are co-created in the image of God and whereas the first human Adam appears to be an earthling, a genderless creature created from the dust of the earth, this is overshadowed by Genesis 2, where the woman, Eve is created out of Adam, co-creating man to be his suitable helper. This story has yielded a myriad of interpretations with dominant ones determining the marginalization of women. To add salt to injury, Genesis 3 is widely taught as depicting Eve as the one who disobeyed God and who led Adam into sin, which has determined the human condition and human mortality. This sealed the curse upon Eve—even if the word "curse" is never used of her in the text itself. Moreover, she has come to signify the reason for oppressing all women after her. Sadly, this has supported and strengthened patriarchal cultures' views and treatment of women as creatures to be dominated and controlled.

Other stories of women in biblical accounts have also served to justify maltreatment of and violence against women and girls. Hence, GBV is all over the Bible, with this chapter describing sample examples. Reading the stories of women's marginalization, subordination, and GBV from the biblical stories of Genesis 1–3, 19, 2 Samuel 13, Esther, and Judges 19 alongside stories of women in Botswana, resonance can be firmly established. In both worlds (the biblical world and contemporary Botswana), women and girls navigate violent conditions that can become lethal. Ultimately, it is not farfetched to suggest that the biblical texts bear some relationship to what is happening in my country, especially given the prominence of the Bible. It is not far-fetched to suggest that biblical stories and motifs promoting female subordination to men, especially when these become affirmed and consolidated with compatible traditional beliefs, contribute to rape culture—that is, the normalization of GBV and sexual violence. Otherwise, one wonders why GBV is thriving in the highly Christianized context of Botswana, where more than 70% of the population subscribes to the religion and where the Bible is held in great awe.

For the same reason—namely, on account of the Bible's tremendous influence—I want to suggest that the Bible also holds potential for addressing GBV. Liberating messages of the Bible are retrievable if we, first, acknowledge and name the rampancy of violence in the text. Rape culture, after all, thrives through normalizing sexual violence and trivializing and misnaming the harm it brings. This makes GBV invisible and mundane instead of inciting our outrage because it shores up the kind of microaggressions and acceptance that lead on to sexual abuse and exploitation, especially of those most vulnerable. Once we identify GBV in biblical texts and speak its name, we can, I believe, redirect these texts towards calling out, labeling as unacceptable, and resisting GBV. Therefore, in the next and final chapter, I want to suggest a reading of the Bible as a mirror reflecting the human condition, including its violence, and then go on to explore its liberating potential.

I see potential for a liberatory reading precisely because there *is* a creation story of equality among humans, alongside the one that has been heard more loudly, because it reappears in an interpretation in the New Testament that has been damaging for women (1 Tim. 2: 11–14). Also, there is in the book of Esther, alongside the large-scale abuse that must be exposed for what it is, the figure of Vashti who speaks up and refuses to be demeaned and objectified. And in the terrible story of Judges 19, the concubine uses her last strength to point (accusingly perhaps) at the threshold of the door from which she was cast out. Likewise, in the awful account of Amnon's rape of Tamar, she, too, does *not* submit—she defends herself. Even after the violence committed against her, Tamar is *not* silent: She cries out in her outrage and righteous agony. These stories of GBV in the Bible are awful stories; they offer familiar glimpses that remind me of the violence I see in my own society and read about often in Botswana's national newspapers. But I also see beyond the descriptions of a shared violent legacy. I believe we can find a name and a focus for our own righteous outrage, and we can insist on the inspirations that are there, both in the Bible and in inspiring people around us, to speak up, speak out, and demand better.

Notes

1 Inter-reading can be and has been practised in African settings with other media for other liberatory purposes. Hence, Adriaan van Klinken et al., 2021. *Sacred Queer Stories: Ugandan LGBTQ+ Refugee Lives and the Bible*, inter-read the life stories of LGBTQ+ refugees in Kenya with Bible stories in an exercise to reclaim the Bible.
2 I will revisit some of this in the final chapter and show that the Bible is rich in ambivalence and lends itself to multiple applications, including to an agenda for liberation from GBV.
3 UNDP, Botswana 2021. Inequality in Botswana.'
4 I am aware that the repercussions of abuse reach even wider. I discuss the connections and interplay between the abuse of women and the environment elsewhere (Kebaneilwe 2015. 'The Good Creation: An Ecowomanist Reading of Genesis; Daniel S., Kebaneilwe M.D., Savala, A. (eds.), 2021. *Mother Earth, Mother Africa and Mission*).
5 It is worth noting that feminists and womanists have been at the helm of bringing these stories to wider attention. These include Phyllis Trible's God and Rhetoric of Sexuality (re Eve) and Texts of Terror (re Tamar and the Levite's Wife), which are pivotal here, as is Weems' Battered Love (re Hosea) and, recently, Ericka Dunbar (re Esther and Vashti). I have already referred to these important publications in the preceding discussion.
6 I am referring to gender binaries in this book because binary gendering (male/female) is the dominant mode in my Botswana context. This has led to binary interpretation of the Bible, too. It is, however, not only true that sex and gender are not either/or, male/female, but also that the creation of 'male and female' here need not mean 'male and female only and nothing else'. Instead, the two named genders could be points along a spectrum.
7 For information on this story, see Thamani Shabani 2020. 'Botswana Still Safe for Women.'
8 The term "fallen" regarding the narrative of Eve in Genesis 1–3 is a Christian designation and used by Carolyn Curtis James (2005: Kindle Edition, 30). She maintains that the view that characterizes Eve as a temptress has led to a fallen view of women in general as morally weak who, if given a chance, would get men in trouble or seize control. Unfortunately, the same suspicion of women, considering them untrustworthy and dangerous, has infested attitudes up to the present. Again, this depiction casts women as both sexual and in need of control, once more tacitly legitimating violence against women. While the Bible is not alone in perpetuating such attitudes, or solely responsible for such attitudes, such do feed into the global human rights scourge of GBV. It is striking that the adjective "fallen" attaches overwhelmingly to women and pertains almost invariably to judgments regarding women's sexual conduct.
9 In Setswana culture, the noun *kgomo* ("cow") is used as a derogatory term for women to emphasize their lack of intelligence, subordination to, and ownership by men. This is widely expressed in proverbs and sayings that belittle women. For instance, if a person, whether male or female, does something signifying stupidity, they are addressed as *yoo ke kgomo* hela, literally translated, "that one is just a

72 Gender-based Violence

mere cow." The word for "bull" is never used as an insult, whereas *kgomo* is applied to demean males and females alike.

10 Phyllis Trible's were not the first, but they do constitute seminal and still oft-cited examples of second-wave feminist interpretations of Genesis 1–3. Including her, 'God *and the Rhetoric of Sexuality*' (1978).

11 I am well aware that this expression is reminiscent of Donald Trump's notorious account and boast, "grab 'em by the pussy." This is yet another example of how powerful and entitled men view women as theirs to exploit.

12 As Thiede illustrates at length, David, as the ultimate hero and masculine man, is himself a consummate rapist.

13 For more information on the amendment, see Botswana Penal Code Amendment 2018.

14 Mpho Mokwape 2021. 'Botswana Records Largest Increase in Defilement Case.'

15 Ibid.

16 Ibid.

17 UNICEF Botswana, 2022. 'COVID-19 Pandemic Exacerbates Existing Vulnerabilities on Children.' 14 March 2022

18 Administrator, the Botswana Gazette, 2022. '5000 Girls Defiled in 2019-21-Police.'

19 Worth noting is that though this title says the girl was a teenager, that is not so since as the story unfolds, it becomes clear that the girl was only 12 years old. This is an indication of how, as already alluded to in the preceding discussions, even media reports do not do justice to the stories concerning women and girls' plight of GBV. There is a tendency to denigrate and treat victims of GBV as though they do not matter hence it is not surprising to see such a misrepresentation as in this case.

20 Cathrine Moemedi 2022. 'Father Defiles Teen Daughter.'

21 Pini Botlhoko 2021. 'BDP Councilor in Hot Soup for Defilement.'

22 Francinah Baaitse 2023. 'SDA Pastor Back in Court for Sex Worker's Murder.'

23 Portia Mlilo 2023. 'Unholy Horror: Apostle Accused of Raping Teen in Church Toilet.'

24 Staff Writer, Mmegi Newspaper 2022. 'Major Kills Private, Turns Rifle on Himself.'

25 Ibid.

26 The third woman is Zeresh, wife of Haman. As Thiede argued of the David story, again, in the book of Esther, men conspire to control and to exploit women, here on a particularly grand scale. The eunuchs are clearly palace officials of some degree of status. Their place in the palace, and in the gender, hierarchy is difficult to establish with certainty.

27 As Barbra Thiede (2022) argues of David, powerful men display their power by means of rape of women. Xerxes demonstrates this on an industrial scale.

28 Pini Botlhoko 2021. 'Crimes of Passion: National Crises.'

29 Ibid.

30 Tshepho Kehimile 2022. 'The Family of the Murdered Teacher Speaks Out.'

31 Moshe Galeragwe 2022. 'Forensic Results Reveal Sexual Assault.

32 In Setswana culture, men are responsible for women's safety: First, as fathers; after marriage, as husbands, in whose absence sons take over the role; or as brothers over their unmarried sisters. The traditional Setswana culture, therefore, is like, if not the same, biblical culture.

33 As is typical of many patriarchal societies, both biblical and Setswana cultures prize women's premarital virginity and insist on women's continence following marriage. The same is not the case for men.

34 It is notable that male characters are rarely held up as archetypes prescribing restrictions on *all* men after them. David may be a model of hegemonic masculinity, but his crimes of adultery, rape, and murder (2 Sam 11) and his punishment (2 Sam 12) are not prominent for being extended up to the present for warning against or

Gender-based Violence 73

curtailing violent men—certainly not in my own experience in Botswana. Again, this shows damaging double standards whereby women and girls are not only victims but victimized, while men are not held to account.

35 This is very different from the co-creation of male and female in Genesis 1, discussed above. Hence, while very many biblical texts suggest a gendered hierarchy in which women are subordinated (sometimes brutally so) to men, the first creation story suggests something quite different and more hopeful.
36 For the full story, see Nnasaretha Kgamanyane 2018. 'Woman Found Beheaded in Tlokweng.'
37 For the full story, see Bonang Mosolotate 2023. 'Man Kills Wife at GBV Centre.'
38 For a full story see, Portia Mlilo 2023. 'Man Found Hanging in Police cells after Killing his Wife.' The Voice, 29 May 2023.
39 For the full story, see Portia Mlilo, 2023. 'Stop Killing Women.'
40 For a more detailed discussion, refer to Musa Dube 2003. 'Culture, Gender and HIV/AIDS.' Dube explains that married women are particularly exposed and vulnerable to HIV because they could not negotiate safe sex with their husbands, with culture barring them from such.
41 UNICEF, Botswana 2022. 'COVID-19 Pandemic Exacerbate Existing Vulnerabilities on children.'
42 For further engagement on the topic of war and GBV, see Helen Liebling-Kalifani et al., 2011. Women War Survivors of the 1989-2003 Conflict in Liberia'; Kostovicova, D. Bojicic-Dzelilovic V. and Henry, M.2020. 'Drawing on the continuum.' These studies' findings also apply to unrest and wars in Botswana's proximity.
43 Neo Kolantsho 2023. 'Killer Son Found Naked near Dead Mum.'
44 Ibid.
45 For a further discussion, see Odireleng Phorano, Keitseope Nthomang, and Dolly Ntseane 2005. 'Alcohol abuse, Gender-based Violence, and HIV/AIDS in Botswana.'
46 For further discussion on the issue of other sexualities implied in Genesis 1, see David M. Carr 2005. '*The Erotic Word.*' Carr argues that 'male' and 'female' need not mean male and female only or procreative sex only. Instead, in reference to the creation of humankind in Genesis 1 and 2, Carr posits that God created the goodness of enduring erotic connectedness between peers/equals, and this is not just between male and female but also includes male-male and female-female relationships.

Bibliography

Administrator, 2022. '5000 Girls Defiled in 2019-21-Police,' The Botswana Gazette Online, 16 November 2022. Available at https://www.thegazette.news/news/5000-girls-defiled-in-2019-21-police/ (Accessed 13 September 2023).

Alter, R., 1980. 'Sacred History and the Beginnings of Prose Fiction.' *Poetics Today* 1(3): 143–162.

Apiko, P., 2019. 'Botswana: One of Africa's Most Stable Democracies but Where Are the Women?' Available at https://ecdpm.org/work/botswana-one-of-africas-most-stable-democracies-but-where-are-the-women (Accessed 12 July 2023).

Baaitse, F., 2023. 'SDA Pastor Back in Court for Sex Worker's Murder,' The Press Reader, 23 January 2023, Available at https://www.pressreader.com/botswana/the-voice-botswana/20230127/281530820154741 and https://zimbabwenow.co.zw/articles/2693/botswana-sda-pastor-up-for-murder-of-zimbabwean-sex-worker (Accessed on 6 June 2023).

74 Gender-based Violence

Bagai, K. and Faimau, G., 2021. Botswana Print Media and the Representation of Female Victims of Intimate Partner Homicide: A Critical Discourse Analytical Approach. *African Journalism Studies*, 42(1):17–35. Available at DOI: 10.1080/23743670.2021.1884581 (Accessed 12 June 2023).

Bailey, R.C., 2020. 'That's Why They Didn't Call the Book Hadassah!': The Interse(ct)/(x)ionality of Race/Ethnicity, Gender, and Sexuality in The Book of Esther.' In Huber, L.R. and Graybill, R. (eds.) *The Bible, Gender, and Sexuality: Critical Readings*. London: Bloomsbury: 167–182.

Bal, M., 1985. Sexuality, Sin and Sorrow: The Emergence of the Female Character (A Reading of Genesis 1-3). *Poetics Today*, 6(1/2): 21–42. https://www.jstor.org/stable/1772119 (Accessed 12 June 2023).

Bauer, G., 2010. 'Cows Will Lead the Herd into a Precipice': Where Are the Women MPs in Botswana?' *Botswana Notes and Records*. 56–70.

Bauer, G., 2016. "What Is Wrong with a Woman Being Chief?" Women Chiefs and Symbolic and Substantive Representation in Botswana.' *Journal of Asian and African Studies* 51(2): 222–237.

Beal, T.K., 1997. *The Book of Hiding: Gender, Ethnicity, Annihilation, and Esther*. New York: Routledge.

Botlhoko, P., 2021b. 'BDP Councilor in Hot Soup for Defilement,' Mmegi Online, 27 September 2021. Available at https://www.mmegi.bw/news/bdp-councillor-in-hot-soup-for-defilement/news (Accessed 13 September 2023).

Botlhoko, P., 2021a. 'Crimes of Passion: National Crises.' Mmegi Online 8 October 2021. Available at https://www.mmegi.bw/news/crimes-of-passion-national-crises/news (Accessed on 6 June 2023).

Botswana Gender-based Violence Briefing Note, 2019. Violence against Women and Girls (VAWG), Helpdesk. Available at https://www.sddirect.org.uk/sites/default/files/2022-10/VAWG-H~1.PDF (Accessed 1 October 2023).

Botswana Penal Code Amendment, 2018. Available at https://www.botswanalaws.com/Botswana2018Pdf/21of2018.pdf (Accessed 12 June 2023).

Carr, D.M., 2005. *The Erotic Word: Sexuality, Spirituality, and the Bible*. Oxford: Oxford University Press.

Clines, D.J., 1990. 'What Does Eve Do to Help? And Other Irredeemably Androcentric Orientations in Genesis 1-3.' In Clines, D.J. (ed.) *What Does Eve Do to Help? And Other Readerly Questions to the Old Testament*. Sheffield: Sheffield Academic Press: 25–48.

Daniel, S., Kebaneilwe, M.D. and Savala, A. (eds.), 2021. *Mother Earth, Mother Africa and Mission*. Stellenbosch: African Sun Media. Available at https://doi.org/10.52779/9781991201317 (Accessed 12 June 2023).

Dube, M.W., 2003a. *Africa Praying: A Handbook on HIV/AIDS Sensitive Sermon Guidelines and Liturgy*. Geneva: WCC.

Dube, M.W. (ed.) 2003b. *HIV/Aids and the Curriculum: Methods of Integrating HIV/AIDS in Theological Programmes*. Geneva: WCC.

Dunbar, E.S., 2021. *Trafficking Hadassah: Collective Trauma, Cultural Memory, and Identity in the Book of Esther and in the African Diaspora*. London: Routledge, Taylor & Francis.

Ellece, S. E., 2011. 'Be a Fool Like Me': Gender Construction in the Marriage Advice Ceremony in Botswana–A Critical Discourse Analysis.' *Agenda* 25(1): 43–52.

Exner, D. and Thurston, W.E., 2009. 'Understanding 'Passion Killings' in Botswana: An Investigation of Media Framing.' *Journal of International Women's Studies* 10(4): 1–16.

Galeragwe, M., 2022. 'Forensic Results Reveal Sexual Assault,' Botswana Daily News, 22 September 2022. Available at https://dailynews.gov.bw/news-detail/69414 (Accessed on 6 June 2023).

James, C.C., 2005. *Lost Women of the Bible: The Women We Thought We Knew*. Grand Rapids, MI: Zondervan.

Kebaneilwe, M. D., 2011. 'The Vashti Paradigm Resistance as a Strategy for Combating HIV.' *The Ecumenical Review* 63(4): 378–383.

Kebaneilwe, M. D., 2012. 'This Courageous Woman: A Socio-rhetorical Womanist Reading of Proverbs 31: 10–31.' PhD diss., Murdoch University. Available at http://researchrepository.murdoch.edu.au/id/eprint/16159 (Accessed 30 September 2023).

Kebaneilwe, M.D., 2015. 'The Good Creation: An Ecowomanist Reading of Genesis 102.' *Old Testament Essays (OTE)* 28(3): 694–703.

Kebaneilwe, M.D., 2018. 'Reading the Book of Esther in the Light of Botswana's 21st-Century Challenges.' *BOLESWA Journal of Theology, Religion and Philosophy (BJTRP)* 5(1): 52–64.

Kehimile, T., 2022. 'The Family of the Murdered Teacher Speaks Out,' The Voice Online, 27 July 2022. Available at https://thevoicebw.com/family-of-murdered-teacher-speaks-out/ (Accessed on 6 June 2023).

Kgamanyane, N., 2018. 'Woman Found Beheaded in Tlokweng,' Mmegi online, 30 July 2018. Available at https://www.mmegi.bw/news/woman-found-beheaded-in-tlokweng/news (Accessed 23 June 2023).

Kolantsho, N., 2023. "Killer Son Found Naked near Dead Mum," The Midweek Sun, 1 February 2023. Available at https://www.pressreader.com/article/281565179903440 (Accessed 13 September 2023).

Kostovicova, D., Bojicic-Dzelilovic, V. and Henry, M., 2020. 'Drawing on the Continuum: A War and Post-war Political Economy of Gender-based Violence in Bosnia and Herzegovina.' *International Feminist Journal of Politics* 22(2): 250–272.

Laverne, M., 2003. *Gill, Vashti's Victory, and Other Women Resisting Injustice*. Cleveland, OH: The Pilgrim Press.

Liebling-Kalifani, H., Mwaka, V., et al., 2011. 'Women War Survivors of the 1989-2003 Conflict in Liberia: The Impact of Sexual and Gender-based Violence.' *Journal of International Women's Studies* 12(1): 1–21.

Low, K.B., 2010. 'The Sexual Abuse of Lot's Daughters: Reconceptualizing Kinship for the Sake of Our Daughters.' *Journal of Feminist Studies in Religion* 26(2): 37–54.

Luke, N. and Kurz, K., 2002. *Cross-Generational and Transactional Sexual Relations in Sub-Saharan Africa*. Washington, DC: International Center for Research on Women (ICRW).

Marsden, D., 2018. *Dishonoured and Unheard: Christian Women and Domestic Violence*. Auckland: Archer Press.

Mlilo, P., 2023a. 'Unholy Horror: Apostle Accused of Raping Teen in Church Toilet,' The Voice Online, 9 May 202. Available at https://thevoicebw.com/unholy-horror/?fbclid=IwAR1RByH-dKYUOAgcYWjfK_WOwecbC_6swhnx01VwgaJTHvXvGfsqU2sQL-0 (Accessed 12 July 2023).

Mlilo, P., 2023b. 'Man Found Hanging in Police Cells after Killing His Wife,' The Voice Online, 29 May 2023. Available at https://thevoicebw.com/man-found-hanging-in-police-cells-after-killing-wife/#:~:text=Molepolole%20police%20Criminal%20Investigation%20Department,Takatokwane%20village%20in%20Kweneng%20west (Accessed 23 September 2023).

Mlilo, P., 2023c. 'Stop Killing Women,' The Voice Online, 5 June 2023. Available at https://thevoicebw.com/stop-killing-women/ (Accessed on 6 June 2023).

Moemedi, C., 2022. 'Father Defiles Teen Daughter,' The Voice Online, 27 September 2022. Available at https://news.thevoicebw.com/father-defiles-teen-daughter/ (Accessed 20 June 2023).

Mogalakwe, M. and Nyamnjoh, F., 2017. 'Botswana at 50: Democratic Deficit, Elite Corruption and Poverty in the Midst of Plenty.' *Journal of Contemporary African Studies 35*(1): 1–14.

Mokwape, M., 2021. 'Botswana Records Largest Increase in Defilement Cases,' Mmegi Online, 5 February 2021. Available at https://www.mmegi.bw/news/botswana-records-largest-increase-in-defilements-cases/news (Accessed 12 June 2023).

Mooketsane, K., Molefe, W. and Faiaz, M. et al. 2023. 'Botswana See Gender-based Violence as a Priority for Government and Societal Action: Afrobarometer Dispatch No. 594.' Available at https://www.afrobarometer.org/wp-content/uploads/2023/01/AD594-Botswana-see-gender-violence-as-a-priority-for-government-and-societal-action-Afrobarometer-18jan23.pdf (Accessed 26 September 2023).

Mookodi, G., 2004. 'The Dynamics of Domestic Violence against Women in Botswana.' *Pula Journal of African Studies 18*(1): 55–64.

Mosolotate, B., 2023. "Man Kills Wife at GBV Centre," Botswana Daily News Online, 25 May 2023. Available at https://dailynews.gov.bw/news-detail/73187 (Accessed 13 September 2023).

Nkomazana, F., 2008. 'The Experiences of Women within Tswana Cultural History and Its Implications for the History of the Church in Botswana.' *Studia Historia Ecclesiasticus 34*(2): 83–119.

Nkosana, J. and Rosenthal, D., 2007. 'The Dynamics of Intergenerational Sexual Relationships: The Experience of Schoolgirls in Botswana.' *Sexual Health 4*(3): 181–187.

Phorano, O., Nthomang, K. and Ntseane, D., 2005. 'Alcohol Abuse, Gender-based Violence and HIV/AIDS in Botswana: Establishing the Link Based on Empirical Evidence.' *SAHARA-J: Journal of Social Aspects of HIV/AIDS 2*(1): 188–202.

Raditloaneng, W.N., 2013. 'An Analysis of Gender-based Domestic Violence and Reactions in Southern Africa.' *Wudpecker Journal of Sociology and Anthropology 1*(5): 60–71.

Ramabu, N.M., 2020. The Extent of Child Sexual Abuse in Botswana: Hidden in Plain Sight. *Heliyon*, 6(4): 1–8. Available at DOI: 10.1016/j.heliyon.2020.e03815 (Accessed 20 July 2023).

Sekano, G.H. and Masango, M.J., 2012. 'In Support of Female Leadership in the Church: Grappling with the Perspective of Setswana Men-Shepherding as Solution Offered.' *Verbum et Ecclesia 33*(1): 1–8.

Shabani, T., 2020. 'Botswana Still Safe for Women,' Daily News, 22 October 2020. Available at https://dailynews.gov.bw/news-detail/59150 (Accessed 24 October 2023).

Shumba, A. and Moorad, F., 2000. 'A Note on the Laws against Child Abuse in Botswana.' *PULA: Botswana Journal of African Studies 15*(2): 253–258.

Singh, M.M., Parsekar, S.S. and Nair, S.N., 2014. 'An Epidemiological Overview of Child Sexual Abuse.' *Journal of Family Medicine and Primary Care* 3(4): e430.
Staff Writer, 2022. 'Major Kills Private, Turns Rifle on Himself,' Mmegi Newspaper, 2 December 2022, Mmegi Online. Available at https://www.mmegi.bw/news/major-kills-private-turns-rifle-on-himself/news (Accessed on 6 June 2023).
Stanton, C.E., 1985. *The Woman's Bible: The Original Feminist Attack on the Bible*. Edinburgh: Polygon Books (Abridgment of the Original Edition). New York: European Publishing Co., 1895, 1898.
Stiebert, J., 2020. *Rape Myths, the Bible, and# MeToo*. London: Routledge, Taylor & Francis.
Thiede, B., 2022. *Rape Culture in the House of David: A Company of Men*. London: Routledge, Taylor & Francis.
Toensing, H.J., 2005. 'Women of Sodom and Gomorrah: Collateral Damage in the War Against Homosexuality?' *Journal of Feminist Studies in Religion* 21(2): 61–74.
Togarasei, L., 2016. 'The Place and Challenges of Modern Pentecostal Christianity in Botswana.' *Botswana Notes and Records* 48: 229–239.
Trible, P., 1978. *God and the Rhetoric of Sexuality* (Vol. 2). Minneapolis: Fortress Press.
Trible, P., 1984. *Texts of Terror: Literary -Feminist Readings of Biblical Narratives*. London: SCM Press.
UNDP, Botswana, 2021. Inequality in Botswana.' Available at https://www.undp.org/sites/g/files/zskgke326/files/migration/bw/UNDP_InequalityInBotswana3_compressed.pdf (Accessed 24 October 2023).
UNICEF Botswana, 2022. 'COVID-19 Pandemic Exacerbate Existing Vulnerabilities on children.' Available at https://www.unicef.org/botswana/press-releases/covid-19-pandemic-exacerbates-existing-vulnerabilities-children (Accessed 1 October 2023).
UN Women: Global Database on Violence Against Women: Statistics from Botswana Police. 2003.' Available at https://evaw-global-database.unwomen.org/en/countries/africa/botswana/2003/statistics-from-the-botswana-police-service (Accessed 23 July 2023).
van Klinken, A., Stiebert, J., Brian Sebyala, B. and Hudson, F., 2021. *Sacred Queer Stories: Ugandan LGBTQ+ Refugee Lives and the Bible*. Oxford: James Currey.
Weiser, S.D., Leiter, K., Bangsberg, D.R., et al., 2007. 'Food Insufficiency Is Associated with High-risk Sexual Behavior among Women in Botswana and Swaziland.' *PLoS Medicine* 4(10): e260.

4 A Way Forward

An Imaginary World with Real People in It: The Bible and the Contemporary World

In his description of how children learn through story reading, James Booth says the following:

> When children read, they understand what the words say to them, translate the experience being read about into their context, and conjure up feelings, attitudes, and ideas concerning everything from the author's values to their own life situations. They react and respond personally, free from outside intervention, and enter as deeply as they decide into this new world, meaning.
>
> (Booth 1985, 193)

This is how reading works. And as children grow into adults, they continue to translate read experience into life situations—particularly so when the literary world is that of the Bible, a text of authority.

In this book, I have attempted to show how the Bible, which has reached and touched communities of faith across the world, is, on the one hand, "just" a literary text, containing narratives, poetry, and laws about ancient societies (particularly ancient Israel) but, on the other, influences the behaviors, attitudes, and actions of real, flesh-and-blood, people. This has had positive and distressing effects, consequences, and potentials.

I have demonstrated how in Botswana the Bible is held in high regard and how, as the sacred text for Christians (with Christianity constituting the country's dominant religion), it has intertwined thoroughly with traditional culture. Thus, the Bible has without doubt proved itself inspirational, transformative, and powerful for Christian Batswana. As part of this, the imaginary-literary world presented in the Bible has gained new life and meaning through the readers and practitioners who have entered deeply and identified with it. The Bible's characters, stories, and content, more generally, have all become enlivened by flesh-and-blood people. In other words, the imaginary has become formative, even a habitat, for real people.

DOI: 10.4324/9781003214137-4

A Way Forward 79

Going back to Booth, Batswana readers not only understand what the words of the Bible say to them but also, importantly, they translate experiences and values transmitted by the text into their own personal life experiences and relate these to their life contexts. The Bible, an old text with long-ago written words, summons feelings, shapes attitudes, incites actions, and has impact in the present including (and maybe especially) in African contexts. No wonder Gerald West (2016) has concluded that the Bible is an African book and icon! Sharing a similar sentiment, Mercy Amba Oduyoye maintains that the Bible is a resource Africans turn to for solutions (Oduyoye 1995, 174). Faith communities in Botswana, too, have adopted, adapted, and translated the Bible, its narratives, teachings, and values into a hybrid of Afro-biblical cultures,[1] creating a powerful creed. Unfortunately, however, the same Bible has been and continues to be used to sustain traditions and customs that suffocate African women (Chitando 2004 152). The coalescence of biblical and African-Setswana patriarchal cultures has seen Batswana women suffocate under the forces of gender-based violence (GBV).

Hegemonic masculinities, heteronormativity, homophobias, and female oppression are no strangers to the worlds portrayed by and in, as well as read into and out from, the Bible, and the same can be found wreaking damage in present-day Botswana, too. Such ills are rampant, and, as this book has shown regarding to GBV, the Bible has provided some of the oxygen for maintaining and enlivening GBV. Importantly, the biblical elements that have negatively influenced and impacted gender relations in Botswana are to a significant degree a result of interpretation. It is, therefore, important to consider that the Bible could also be *differently* engaged to facilitate interpretations with more positive outcomes, aimed at more desirable transformations, in this case, targeting GBV.

The nature of the Bible, given its sparse narrations and many ambiguities, is such that it lends itself to multiple interpretations, and so, it offers multiple interpretive opportunities for its readers, practitioners, and communities of faith. Inasmuch as it has been read to support behaviors, attitudes, and actions that are violent towards certain groups, as has been the case for both Lesbian Gay Bisexual Transgender Queer (LGBTQ+) communities in Uganda and elsewhere (see Kuloba 2016 *passim*) and for the subordination of women in many parts of Africa, including in Botswana, the Bible can also be read and explored in ways that are powerfully affirmative and life-giving (van Klinken and Muyunga-Mukasa 2021).

Noteworthy, even notorious, is that the Bible is applied to support competing and even contradictory discourses that can build up or tear down. A typical example is the creation of human beings in Genesis 1:27 and Genesis 2:21–23. As noted in Chapter 3, the two texts confront the reader with two distinct versions of how the first humans came into being. The question then is whether one should go with the first version (Genesis 1:27), which presents both male and female (and maybe more) as created simultaneously, or with the second version, in Genesis 2, which gives the impression that the man was created first while the woman was created later, from a part of the man and to be his *helper*. As I have already indicated, the latter version has been given preference in the dominant interpretation of these texts, over the former (and certainly in Botswana). Moreover, interpretation has imposed a hierarchy of being on the order of creation, with primacy of the man's creation rendering the woman inferior, derivative, and secondary. I have no doubt that this has contributed to the marginalization, subordination, and oppression of women and to the rampancy of GBV in my context. Batswana men have used such texts to justify and uphold Setswana traditions and cultural mores that show little regard for women. In this way, the Bible and Setswana tradition have cohered in toxic ways, with each propping up select toxic elements of the other.

My suggestion in this book is that to achieve gender justice, there is urgent need to change the dominant and damaging ways the Bible has been interpreted especially by church authorities—who are predominantly male, as I demonstrated in Chapter 2. The church, certainly in Botswana, has avoided confronting such social ills as the widespread existence of GBV inherent in both biblical materials and present-day society. There has been a lot of spiritualizing of that which is violent in biblical texts: Such as the marginalization of othered groups, women and girls, and LGBTQ+ persons. Such texts have been justified as defining Christian morality/ethics while indeed, as shown throughout this book, they support a status quo favoring and upholding hegemonic male supremacy and domination. The moral compass has shrunk to "the Bible says ..." Without adequate questioning, reflection, and probing. For example, 1 Timothy 2:11–13 and 1 Corinthians 14:34 deny women a voice in church and order them to remain silent and in submission to male authority. These verses have been used as strategies to keep women in subservient positions, including in contemporary African settings, as observed by Ezra Chitando (2019, 20–21). This has disadvantaged women in numerous ways, denying them leadership positions not only in the church but also in the political sector, and other public and even private places. And this has led to a situation where in Botswana authority is now concentrated in the hands of men (see Chapter 2). Such texts, and others like them, have been read in isolation, magnified, and weaponized against women and girls. Once again, one manifestation of this has been GBV, as demonstrated throughout this book.

While my focus has been GBV against women, I want to refer to a recent incident in Botswana that shows how biblical texts have been used violently in Botswana to promote a culture that marginalizes and oppresses also other non-hegemonic groups, such as members of the LGBTQ+ community. In a newspaper report titled "Churches Protest Against Bill on Homosexuality," it is stated thus:

> Religious leaders from the Evangelical Fellowship of Botswana (EFB) led a demonstration on Saturday to hand over an appeal to Parliament against a bill, which seeks to legitimize homosexual same-sex practices in the

country .... The Bible clearly abhors homosexuality, and it is the duty of EFB to take the biblical stand that the practice, in whatever form, is sinful and unacceptable.

(Matlala 2023)

The above extract demonstrates explicitly that the Bible has been applied as though it is an incontestable text containing a holy creed that can be plainly understood and must be followed without question. But this is not the case. I have acknowledged the strides achieved in this regard, especially by biblical scholars who have engaged critically with biblical discourses, revealing their ideologies. Such efforts include those of feminist and womanist scholars for instance—including in southern Africa (see Chapter 2). However, as indicated, a lot still needs to be done to undo rigid mindsets and the uncritical reading or acceptance of biblical texts. Therefore, I propose that if the Bible is to achieve effective transformation for the betterment of humanity, especially in communities of faith such as in Botswana, where it is accepted as an authoritative text, then it must be acknowledged as mirroring the human condition in its full range, including human brutality. This cannot be hidden, ignored, covered up, or spiritualized away. It needs, instead, to be confronted and then challenged.

The Bible is confrontational in that it reflects parts of life we may not want to acknowledge or admit to jealousy, murderous desire, passion, anger, and violence. Worse still, as biblical scholars have acknowledged for some time, the Bible is androcentric, and sometimes misogynistic; it is a product of male authorship, mostly featuring male protagonists (Bird 1997; Kebaneilwe and Ellece 2020; Meyers 1998). It portrays a patriarchal world characterized by male domination over women and other non-hegemonic groups.

The Bible presents a world in which competition, aggression, greed, and survival of the strongest prevail. For example, Genesis 4 (the story of Cain's jealousy-motivated murder of his brother Abel), Genesis 30 (Rachel and Leah's rivalry and competition), Genesis 37 (where Joseph angers his brothers), Exodus 32 (where an angry Moses punishes the Israelites), John 12: 4–6 (featuring a deceitful Judas Iscariot), 2 Samuel 11 (depicting David's lust for Bathsheba), and numerous others. It is also inherently misogynist; for example, in Genesis 19, Lot offers up his daughters to a threatening mob—an action that is never criticized in the text itself and for which some commentators through the ages have praised Lot, for his hospitality. Or Judges 19, where a Levite's concubine is sacrificed to save men. She is gang-raped all night and later dismembered. As Chapter 3 shows, GBV is rampant in biblical texts as it is in real life in Botswana. In a nutshell, the Bible's controversial patriarchal tendencies are revealed through its narratives. In the biblical stories I focused on in the preceding chapter, hegemonic male rule, in which stronger males are the heroes who determine the destinies and fates of others, including women and girls, is commonplace. Such a situation is visible also in the contemporary world as demonstrated through GBV narratives from Botswana. But the presence of these texts need not provide templates and weapons. If we don't hide from or spiritualize them, these texts, for all their horror, give us a medium to reflect on and better to critique violence and injustice.

In the narrative of 2 Samuel 13, David's daughter Tamar is raped by her half-brother Amnon. An array of emotions may have motivated Amnon, including lust, greed, self-centeredness, and a desire to dominate both his sister and their popular brother, Absalom. Whatever the case, Tamar, a beautiful girl, is ultimately an object to be used and abused by males. She is terribly abused by Amnon, but she is also let down by her father (who does nothing), by her brother Absalom (who tells her to keep quiet), by her cousin Jonadab (who conspires to facilitate her ruin), and by Amnon's household servants (none of whom intervenes on her behalf). A reader sensitive to issues of GBV sees something much more sinister and systemic in this story than a depraved rapist, who might be dismissed as "one bad apple." It is clear from the *male* conversation that transpires prior to the rape (2 Samuel 13: 1–10), that neither Amnon nor his (and Tamar's) cousin "loves" Tamar as the text purports of Amnon (v. 1). The narrative also, however, reflects something of the real, intimate, and very painful experiences of countless sexually violated women and girls in Botswana and elsewhere (Chapter 3). This is because we receive some insight into Tamar: Her words of resistance before the rape and her cries of anguish after the rape are recorded in the narrative. Thus, looking at this text, I see the reflection of my context and of the wickedness committed against us, Batswana women, who live, like Tamar, in misogynistic and patriarchal worlds. As I reflect on Tamar's ordeal, not only do I see her story's biblical characters but also, I see the men and boys of my own community, some of whom prey on women and girls. I hear the cries of countless Batswana women and girls whose bodies and vaginas are grabbed, used, and disposed of by cruel men and boys. Indeed, the text is in this case a mirror through which I can see my own world and the realities of GBV, and its place in the Bible gives me a way to grieve and an impetus to call for change and for justice. I can point to the perpetrators and to their wickedness by pointing at the text; I can point to Tamar and to the appalling devastation rape causes—and I can and do demand justice, on the authority of the Bible itself, no less.

Another example is that of King Xerxes, a powerful man who ruled over 127 provinces (Esther 1: 1–2) and who abused his authority to subject all others, notably women and girls from every province, to feed his arrogance, lust, and greed. He surrounded himself with sycophantic servants and with eunuchs (Esther 1:10) to make himself feel powerful. When his wife, Queen Vashti, dared to protect her dignity by refusing to parade naked before him and his male drinking companions (Esther 1:11; 12, and 19), she is deposed and evicted, which has consequences for all women in the empire.

Again, Vashti's ordeal can mirror the ordeals of women in Botswana, reflecting what can befall women who refuse to submit to their husbands.

I have demonstrated that many homicides, or better, femicides in Botswana, are explained by perpetrators as crimes of "passion" or as deriving from "frustration" at women's lack of subservience. Like their biblical sister Vashti, who suffers textual death when her story ends with her banishment from the palace (Esther 1:19), Batswana women are literally violated and killed for trying to speak up or defend themselves. Rates of intimate partner violence in Botswana are high and perpetrators are predominantly men, many of whom feel justified in exerting their greater physical power over women. In the Esther story, women are treated as property of men: Hence, Esther is taken into the King's harem together with countless other young virgin girls (Esther 2:8–9). And there are other accounts of male control over their wives in the Bible, such as Numbers 5, where a law decrees that a jealous man has the latitude to make his wife drink poison, if he so much as *suspects* that his wife was unfaithful to him. This indicates that the men reflected in biblical accounts had power over women, power that could transpire in heinous and inhuman acts against the women under their control. Again, this can give us a way to reflect together on real life in Botswana, to recognize what is wrong, and to resist (like Vashti).

The biblical GBV incidences perpetrated by textual men and boys on textual women and girls can bring us to reflect on real flesh-and-blood people living in twenty-first century Botswana. While Botswana has been used as the case study for this book to substantiate my argument that the Bible can be a resource for examining and for making a difference in real life, this could be and has been applied to other places also.

I have demonstrated in the previous chapters how beginning with the story of Eve in the book of Genesis, women have been treated with contempt and suspicion and consequently been mistreated. I have shown that rape abounds in the Bible and that women and girls are disproportionately affected as victims; this is tragically true of my own context, Botswana, with its extremely high rates of sexual violence. I have also referred to the complicity of some Bible—using faith leaders who are often male and use the Bible to maintain a patriarchal status quo. I have also cited the case where a group of churches protested the possibility of a bill allowing equal rights and opportunities for non-heterosexual people in Botswana to pass into law. As a biblical scholar investigating the Bible, which holds such considerable authority in my country, I see a resource for reflecting on the contemporary world, particularly the reasons for and impact of GBV. Failure to see and resist GBV, either in the Bible or in my context where the Bible is ever-present, is a failure to do what is right and seek justice, particularly for vulnerable women and girls.

The scenario of a mirror reflection where one looks into the mirror and sees themselves, acknowledging what they see, serves in the following two significant ways:

1 If one looks into the mirror and sees that they need to fix some things about themselves (e.g., their hair or any shirt buttons placed in the wrong holes),

acknowledging that and acting on it help the person become presentable or better. It also teaches them to keep up this practice so that they can continue to do so and be better also going forward.
2 But if, on the contrary, one looks into the mirror, sees that their face is messy from the food they may just have eaten, then chooses to ignore, or disregard, or justify their inaction, then they will not only display their own mess but also show it to others, and be more likely to keep this up going forward, forming a habit. Thus, because they fail to see and act on the mirror reflection of themselves, they cannot benefit from the possible transformative effects of the mirror. The mirror is no longer, for them, a useful tool for correction.

This may be a banal example, but there is a bigger point I am trying to make. Like a mirror, the Bible is an accessible resource—but only if we first *use it* and, second, use it *purposefully and constructively with integrity*. This applies also to faith communities in Christianized contexts like Botswana. I have noted that the tendency has been to select from the Bible texts that support the status quo shaped also by the Setswana tradition of androcentrism that has facilitated the domination of girls and women and promoted the scourge of GBV against them. The Bible, while it can offer texts and tools for justice, has not always helped to address GBV in Botswana settings because, even though looking into its pages provides resonances with incidents of GBV in our country, the tendency has been to deny and ignore this and to continue promoting the causes of GBV, such as male domination and female submission. I suggest that allowing the biblical text to exercise alternative transformational effects to change our world for the better could go some way towards eliminating GBV. But for this to happen, we must first acknowledge and reflect on the harmful depictions in biblical pages. The second step is to judge, as beings endowed with the power of reason, what is best, what is liberating, and what is inclusive for the benefit of all. The final step is to learn to put into action what is good—and here, the Bible, used as a mirror, can offer us resources, too.

Note

1 I use African cultures and not culture to highlight that Africa is a vast continent with diverse and numerous peoples and cultures. The Bible, too, written as it was over several centuries, contains traces of multiple cultures.

Bibliography

Bird, P.A., 1997. 'The Place of Women in the Israelite Cultus.' In Bach, A. (ed.) *Women in the Hebrew Bible*. New York: Routledge: 3–20.
Booth, D., 1985. '"Imaginary Gardens with Real Toads": Reading and Drama in Education.' *Theory into Practice* 24(3): 193–198.

Chitando, E., 2004. 'The Good Wife: A Phenomenological Re-reading of Proverbs 31: 10-31 in the Context of HIV/Aids in Zimbabwe.' *Scriptura: Journal for Contextual Hermeneutics in Southern Africa* 86(1): 151–159.
Chitando, E., 2019. 'Introduction: The Bible, the Church, and Gender Troubles in Africa.' In Kügler, J., Gabaitse, R. and Stiebert, J. (eds.) *The Bible and Gender Troubles in Africa* (Vol. 22). Bamberg: University of Bamberg Press: 13–24.
Kebaneilwe, M.D. and Ellece, S., 2020. 'The Untold Story of "Mrs Noah": The Hebrew Bible, Gender, and Media: An Intertextual Critical Discourse Analysis.' *Boleswa Journal of Theology, Religion and Philosophy (BJTRP)* 5*(2)*: 32–48.
Kuloba, R.W., 2016. "Homosexuality Is Unafrican and Unbiblical": Examining the Ideological Motivations to Homophobia in Sub-Saharan Africa–The Case Study of Uganda.' *Journal of Theology for Southern Africa* 154: 6–27.
Matlala, K., 2023. 'Church Protest Against Bill on Homosexuality,' Botswana Daily News, 24 July 2023. Available at https://dailynews.gov.bw/news-detail/74193 (Accessed on 17 Sep 2023).
Meyers, C.L., 1998. 'Everyday Life: Women in the Period of the Hebrew Bible.' In Newsom, C.A. and Ringe, S.H. (eds.) *Women's Bible Commentary*. Louisville: Westminster Press: 244–251.
Newsom, C.A. and Ringe, S.H. (eds.) 1998. *Women's Bible Commentary*. Louisville: Westminster Press.
Oduyoye, M.A., 1995. 'Christianity and African Culture.' *International Review of Mission* 84(332–333): 77–90.
van Klinken, A. and Muyunga-Mukasa, T., 2021. '"Accused of a Sodomy Act": Bible, Queer Poetry and African Narrative Hermeneutics.' *Journal for Interdisciplinary Biblical Studies* 2(2): 25–46.
van Klinken, A., Stiebert, J., Brian, S. and Fredrick, H., 2021. *Sacred Queer Stories: Ugandan LGBTQ+ Refugee Lives and the Bible*. Surrey: James Currey.
West, G.O., 2016. *The Stolen Bible: From Tool of Imperialism to African Icon* (Vol. 144). Leiden: Brill.

Index

Note: Page references with "n" denote endnotes.

2 Samuel 13 and rape narratives from Botswana 56–61, 70, 82

African cultures 45n15, 84n1
Afro-biblical cultures 79

Badimo 19–21
Bailey, Randall 61, 65
banishments 61–64
barred choices 61–64
Batswana men 9, 19; Christian norms 22; in church leadership 42; derogatory comments 2; socialization 22; and women 42, 68, 80; and women's bodies 42
Batswana women 4, 7, 10, 13, 18–19, 63–66; and Batswana men 42, 68, 80; and Botswana's patriarchal culture to 54; empowering 42; Setswana gender ideologies 49; socialization 22; violations/killings of 83; *see also* women/girls
Beal, T.K. 65
Berman, Sidney 41–42
Bible 49, 71n6, 71n8, 84n1; confronting patriarchal status quo 38–43; and contemporary world 78–84; and GBV 32–44; gender inequality 22; heuristic ways of reading and interpreting 1; importance in Botswana 1; many faces of GBV in 66–69; on wartime rape 32–33

The Bible and Gender Troubles in Africa 37–38
biblical texts 43–44; 2 Samuel 13 and rape narratives from Botswana 56–61; The Book of Esther and GBV in Botswana 61–64; deposition of females/GBV 52–54; endemic in 49–71; Eve and GBV 54–56; female bodies for male desire/gratification 64–66; GBV in Bible and Botswana 66–69; Genesis 1–3 52–54; grabbing of vaginas 56–61; and intimate partner violence (IPV) 55; objectification and sexualization 64–66; ordinary readers on 34; and Ujamaa Centre 33–38; women's bodies as spaces of contention 66–69; *see also* Bible
biblical war narratives 32–33
Blyth, Caroline 33
The Book of Esther: banishments 61–64; barred choices 61–64; and GBV in Botswana 61–64; silencing 61–64
Booth, James 78–79
Borramogolwane 20
Botswana: 2 Samuel 13 and rape narratives from 56–61; background 4–7; Christianity in 20–22, 25; cultural landscape of 11–13; GBV crisis in 1–2; grabbing of vaginas 56–61; importance of Bible 1; independence 5; many faces of GBV in 66–69;

missionaries in 7, 22, 56;
    passion killings 3; religious
    landscape of 19–24; silencing/
    barred choices/banishments
    61–64; socio-political
    landscape of 11–13
Botswana Constitution: discrimination
    based on gender 13–14;
    Domestic Violence Act (2008)
    14–19
The Botswana Daily News 51, 54
Botswana Democratic Party (BDP) 5, 60
The Botswana Gazette 51
Botswana Penal Code 58
Botswana Police Service 59, 62

Cailleba, P. 11, 16
Carr, David M. 73n46
child sexual abuse 3, 56, 59
Chitando, Ezra 38, 80
Christian Batswana 78
Christianity 1–2, 7, 78; and African
    Traditional Religion 20;
    in Botswana 20–22, 25;
    colonization 25; denominations
    of 19; patriarchal perceptions
    24; in South Africa 35; spread
    of 20; *see also* Bible; biblical
    texts
Christian morality/ethics 80
Citizenship Act (1982) 15
Colgan, Emily 33
common law 11, 13, 17–18, 25
community discord 59
Contextual Bible Study (CBS) 34, 49
*Contextual Bible Study Manual on
    Gender-based Violence* 35
COVID-19 pandemic 59, 68
customary law 9, 11, 14, 18, 25

Denbow, James 7
discrimination based on gender 13–14
Domestic Violence Act (2008) 14–19;
    Abolition of Marital Power
    Act of 2004 17–19; Penal
    Code of Botswana amendment
    16; Sexual Harassment Act
    16–17
Dube, Musa 39–40, 73n40
Dunbar, Ericka 62, 65

Edwards, Katie 33
Emang Basadi 15, 26n20

endemic in biblical texts 49–71
'*The Erotic Word*' (Carr) 73n46
Evangelical Fellowship Botswana (EFB)
    12
Eve: embodiment of *fallen* model
    for all women 54–56; and GBV
    54–56

"The Fellowship of Christian Councils
    and Churches in the Great
    Lakes and the Horn of Africa"
    (FECCLAHA) 35
female(s): beginning of deposition
    of 52–54; oppression of 19,
    23–25, 36, 39–40, 42, 79–80;
    subordination of 23–24, 40–41,
    51, 70; *see also* women/girls
female bodies: for male desire/
    gratification 64–66;
    objectification of 64–66;
    sexualization of 64–66

Gabaitse, Rosinah 23, 40–41
"Gender, Power, Sexuality and Suffering
    Bodies in the Book of Esther"
    (Nadar) 36
gender-based violence (GBV) 1, 49–71,
    72n19, 79; archetype 54–56;
    beginning of deposition of
    52–54; and Bible 32–44; crisis
    in Botswana 1–2, 6; defining
    3–4; many faces in Bible
    66–69; many faces in Botswana
    66–69; silencing/barred choices/
    banishments 61–64
gender inequality: Bible 22; in Botswana
    6–7; Pentecostal churches 23
gender justice 36–37, 41, 50, 80
gender roles 24; in Botswana 7–8;
    Setswana marriage 8; Setswana
    proverbs 8–11
Genesis 1–3 52–54
globalization 39–40
Grace, Obagboye 15

Hebrew Bible 69
hegemonic masculinity 57–58,
    72n34, 79
heteronormativity 51, 79
HIV/AIDS pandemic 39–40, 45n14,
    63, 68
homicides 62–63, 83
homophobias 79

intimate partner homicides (IPH) 56
intimate partner violence (IPV) 55

James, Carolyn Curtis 54, 71n8

Kagisano Society 15
Kairos Document 33
Kenya: GBV in 35; LGBTQ+ refugees in 71n1; Tamar Campaign in 35, 61
kgotla 9
King Xerxes 61–65, 82
Kügler, Joachim 37
Kumar, R.A. 11, 16

Lesbian, Gay, Bisexual, Transgender, Intersex and Queer persons (LGBTIQ+) 12
Lesbians, Gays & Bisexuals of Botswana LEGABIBO vs. The Attorney General 12, 26n12
LGBTQ+ communities: in Botswana 80; in Uganda 79
Livingstone, David 20
Low, Katherine 66

male desire/gratification 64–66
male supremacy 23–25, 41, 51, 80
Masenya, Madipoane 36, 49
Maundeni, Tapologo 15
microaggressions 70
missionaries 7, 22, 56
Mmegi 51, 59, 62, 67
Modimo (God) 20
Moffat, Robert 7
Montgomery, Taryn 35
Mosadi, Kgosi Seboko 9
Motswana: Christian 22; defined 25n2; women 1, 9

Nadar, Sarojini 36, 49
New Testament 40, 55, 70
Nkomazana, Fidelis 21, 56
The No. 1 Ladies Detective Agency (Smith) 2
Ntlo ya Dikgosi ("House of Chiefs") 9–10
Nyabera, Fred 35

objectification: female bodies 64–66; and sexualization 64–66
Oduyoye, Mercy Amba 79
ordinary readers: on biblical texts 34; defined 34

passion killings 3, 13, 63
"Passion Killings in Botswana: Masculinity at Crossroads" (Gabaitse) 40–41
patriarchy 10–11, 19–24, 45n13, 54, 64
Pentecostal churches 23
Phyllis Trible 72n10

Quansah, Emmanuel 4, 19

rape: cultures 2, 7, 10, 17, 33, 52, 61–62, 70; narratives from Botswana 56–61; spousal 16; wartime 32–33
Rape Culture, Gender Violence and Religion: Biblical Perspectives 33
Rape Culture in the House of David: A Company of Men (Thiede) 33
Rape Myths, the Bible, and #MeToo 33

Sacred Queer Stories: Ugandan LGBTQ+ Refugee Lives and the Bible 71n1
Setswana culture 54, 59, 71n9, 72n32, 72n33; confronting patriarchal status quo 38–43; gender roles and marriage 8; proverbs and gender roles 8–11; and tradition 56
Setswana patriarchal culture 21, 56, 79
sexual abuse 56; child 3, 56, 59; gendered 56; and microaggressions 70
Sexual Harassment Act 16–17
sexualization, of female bodies 64–66
sexual violence 2–4, 34, 43, 50, 56–58, 60, 70, 83; *see also* rape
silencing 61–64
Smith, Alexander McCall 2
South Africa: Bible and GBV 35–36; decriminalizing consensual homosexual sex acts 26n12; ethnic and racial groups in 45n13; Pentecostal churches in 23; political crisis in 33; progressive constitution of 4; San people in 4; Tamar Campaign in 61; Ujamaa Centre 33–38; women rape in 4

spousal rape 16
Stanton, Elizabeth 53
Stiebert, Johanna 52
The Sunday Standard 51

"Talita Cum: Calling the Girl-Child and Women to Life in the HIV and Globalization Era" (Dube) 39
Tamar Campaign 34–35; in Kenya 35, 61; in South Africa 61
Texts of Terror: Literary-Feminist Readings of Biblical Narratives (Trible) 44n8
Thebe, Phenyo 7
Thiede, Barbara 33, 57, 58, 61, 72n12, 72n26, 72n27
Trible, Phyllis 44n8
Trump, Donald 72n11

Uganda: Lesbian Gay Bisexual Transgender Queer (LGBTQ+) communities in 79
Ujamaa Centre 33–38
UN General Assembly 3
UNICEF 59
UNICEF Botswana 68
United Nations Development Program (UNDP) 50

"The Untold Story of 'Mrs Noah': The Hebrew Bible, Gender and Media: An Intertextual Critical Discourse Analysis" (Kebaneilwe and Ellece) 42

violence: gender-based (*see* gender-based violence (GBV)); intimate partner 55; sexual 2–4, 34, 43, 50, 56–58, 60, 70, 83
The Voice 51, 60

West, Gerald 34, 79
"Without a Voice, with a Violated Body: Re-reading Judges to Challenge Gender-based Violence in Sacred Texts" (Masenya) 36
women/girls: and Batswana men 42, 68, 80; bodies as spaces of contention 66–69; as "cows" 56; embodiment of *fallen* model for all 54–56; and GBV 2; and GBV in Bible and Botswana 66–69; as *kgomo* ("cow") 71–72n9; oppression of 19, 23–25, 36, 39–40, 42, 79–80; rape in South Africa 4; as sexual object 2; *see also* Batswana women

For Product Safety Concerns and Information please contact our EU
representative GPSR@taylorandfrancis.com
Taylor & Francis Verlag GmbH, Kaufingerstraße 24, 80331 München, Germany

www.ingramcontent.com/pod-product-compliance
Lightning Source LLC
Chambersburg PA
CBHW051759230426
43670CB00012B/2351